PARANORMAL ENCOUNTERS ON BRITAIN'S ROADS

PARANORMAL ENCOUNTERS ON BRITAIN'S ROADS

PHANTOM FIGURES, UFOs AND MISSING TIME

PETER A. McCUE

The History Press

Cover illustration: Martin Latham

First published 2018

The History Press
The Mill, Brimscombe Port
Stroud, Gloucestershire, GL5 2QG
www.thehistorypress.co.uk

British Library Cataloguing in Publication Data.
A catalogue record for this book is available from the British Library.

ISBN 978 0 7509 8438 6

Typesetting and origination by The History Press
Printed and bound by CPI Group (UK) Ltd

CONTENTS

ACKNOWLEDGEMENTS

I should like to thank Ron Halliday for kindly writing the Foreword to this book. I am grateful to David T. Muir and David Haith for their help with proofreading. I am appreciative of the people who have given me accounts of their strange experiences. Special thanks go to Sean Tudor, for providing information about the Blue Bell Hill apparitions and for permission to use two of his photographs of the area. I'd also like to thank Kevin Goodman, for his photograph of Oldnall Road in the West Midlands, and David Feast, for his photograph of Colloway Clump, Warminster. I'm also grateful to the following, for providing information or assistance: Kathleen Cronie, Rob Gandy, Steve Mera, Alan Murdie, David Taylor, Danielle Thompson and Steve Wills.

FOREWORD

For centuries individuals – and since the nineteenth century various investigative organisations, the best known being the Society for Psychical Research – have striven to make sense of claims of encounters with 'phantoms', 'ghosts' and 'spirits', entities whose appearance defies, or certainly seems to defy, at first glance, our rational, scientific world.

In *Paranormal Encounters on Britain's Roads: Phantom Figures, UFOs and Missing Time*, the author, Dr Peter McCue, has assembled a fascinating array of reported encounters with apparitions from all corners of Great Britain. The spread of sightings is remarkable and begs the question of the nature of the phenomena (or is it phenomenon?) that we are dealing with. It is a formidable challenge to seek to make sense of events of a quite extraordinary nature, but in this work Dr McCue has shed light on one particular aspect the curious phenomenon of encounters with ghosts on the UK's road network, which may, in its turn, have broader implications for the investigation of apparitions.

It is heartening to note that Dr McCue opens his book with a definition of terms regularly used by those investigating and writing about the paranormal. It is useful both as a guide to the accepted meaning of these terms and in that it makes clear the context in which the author is using these expressions. It gives considerable clarity to the examples he cites and the discussion he gives in relation to these events. One wishes that other authors would be equally explicit, as one of the problems the reader faces when working through a narrative is to be sure that reader and author are on the same wavelength when certain technical terms are being frequently used. Those already versed in the subject will find some of the terms used familiar, for example, *extrasensory perception (ESP)* and *telepathy* – nomenclature that has been in use for many years. Others less so, and I mention *retrocognition*, a term I admit I was unfamiliar with, which demonstrates that one can always learn.

In his book, Dr McCue has focused on those sightings of apparitions which have been witnessed on or in relation to roads. To his credit, he has also tackled the controversial subject of 'Unidentified Flying Objects' or 'UFOs'. As he states, quite rightly in my view, 'Some UFO sightings may be apparitional events.' I can readily confirm that descriptions of UFOs related to me by witnesses bear a definite resemblance to ghost encounters. The object can, for example, be almost wisp-like or translucent, similar to the traditional ghost. On the other hand, UFOs can appear solid – like real nuts-and-bolts machines – and appear to support the belief of some enthusiasts that we are dealing with an alien race of space travellers. However, let us not forget that apparitions – in spite of the subjective inference of the word – can also appear solid as, for example, cases involving the 'phantom hitchhiker' reveal, as described by Dr McCue. A fascinating and, one might add, particularly disturbing aspect of the ghost encounter. If a phantom can appear solid and interact meaningfully with its or our surroundings, it raises fundamental questions about the nature of our reality. It doesn't, if one can be frank, appear to make much sense; but, even so, perfectly rational people, with no axe to grind, have claimed to encounter 'ghosts' which appear no different in substance than you or I. It's a paradox which appears to defy an obvious explanation. Or at least a solution on which there is broad agreement, as there are almost as many different views on the matter as there are writers and investigators! Dr McCue doesn't avoid these issues, and delivers a stimulating discussion of the theories put forward to account for the appearance of apparitions and other phenomena, such as alleged alien abduction. He explains the difference between a 'theory' and a 'hypothesis', a separation which is frequently confused by writers on the supernatural, but an important difference to be aware of when assessing the validity of the paranormal experience.

It's well established that, as Dr McCue puts it, 'Some people seem to be especially prone to unusual experiences.' These individuals are known in UFO-speak as 'repeater witnesses', although having more than one paranormal experience certainly isn't confined to UFO sightings. Dr McCue examines this issue in relation to UFO abductees. Why do some people have encounters which defy everyday experience and have them more than once? Is there something unusual about these individuals, as you might expect there to be? It appears not to be the case. As Dr McCue recounts, studies conducted on UFO abductees, comparing them with control subjects, discovered 'no significant differences between them regarding factors such as emotional intelligence, fantasy-proneness, extraversion, emotional stability, and openness to experience'. This is a surprising conclusion but I would add that it chimes with my own experience of interviewing abductees and others who claim to have had an encounter of a paranormal nature. These individuals usually were not looking for anything odd to happen to them and saw themselves as 'ordinary' people who had had an extraordinary experience, one that was frequently viewed as unsettling and even unpleasant.

That does not, of course, mean that supposedly inexplicable experiences involve the supernatural. It's a 'taken' amongst UFO investigators that 90 per cent or more of UFO sightings can be explained by natural phenomena – for example, misidentification of aircraft or planets, reflection of ground lights into the sky, and so on. One view held by sceptics is that if we had all the information about a paranormal encounter, we would be able to explain every incident in a rational way. It's also suggested that the volume of sightings doesn't mean the phenomenon exists – an argument put forward in relation to the Loch Ness Monster, for example. These views have to be taken seriously, but to counter that, one has cases, for example, of close encounters, of highly detailed incidents which are harder to explain away by supposed lack of information, an argument which I feel tends towards an intellectual 'cop out'.

I won't enumerate the large number of strange encounters given by Dr McCue – that's what reading the book is for! There are far too many to describe, but they are all fascinating in their own way. The 'disappearing car' phenomenon is well documented, but unnerving nonetheless. Here we have a car which hurtles towards you, you swerve to avoid it, and then – glancing in your rear-view mirror – discover that the vehicle has vanished. This – among many others – is one aspect of the ghost phenomenon which puzzles me. Why do 'phantoms' appear solid but then 'dematerialise'? Incidents from across the UK, as documented by Dr McCue, including ghost planes, demonstrate the geographical extent and significant incidence of this class of event. In each chapter, Dr McCue provides useful comments, giving his own view of the various phenomena.

An astonishing variety of objects have been encountered on Britain's roads, including alien big cats, phantom black dogs, mysterious light phenomena plus vehicle interference. All of these types of incidents, and more, Dr McCue has examined in detail. The variety of incidents is remarkable: a cyclist colliding with phantom horses, a motorist running over a smiling woman on a road in Kent, feeling the impact of the collision, but no one being found there, even following a search conducted by the police. How can one explain such an occurrence?

There have been a surprising number of phantom beast sightings reported by motorists. I've certainly interviewed witnesses to such encounters. Interestingly, Dr McCue cites an example of a sighting at Rendlesham Forest, the location of a well-known UFO incident. It's been suggested by other writers that phantom beasts and UFOs are connected in some way, though that appears as little more than wild speculation. It may be that on some occasions genuine big cats may have been encountered, and Dr McCue cites a case in which 'a black creature with massive teeth' crashed into the side of a car, leaving 'a huge dent'.

Phantom beasts have a long pedigree. Before the appearance of 'black cats', phantom black dogs were frequently reported. Dr McCue devotes a chapter to the 'black dog' phenomenon, reporting a supposed incident from as far back as 1577. Such is the fame of the phantom black dog in Suffolk, following that legendary encounter, that the creature appears on the town of Bungay's coat of arms. As Dr McCue establishes, the sightings of the phantom black dog are too frequent and well documented to dismiss. But how do we account for them? Dr McCue once again seeks to provide us with explanations to consider, including the possibility that 'unconsciously and via ESP, the people concerned learned they were in danger, and … somehow created the apparitional dogs themselves', an intriguing idea.

In his admirable 'conclusion', Dr McCue draws attention to several issues. As he points out, the number of reported cases is simply that – *reported* incidents. It is impossible to know how many encounters go unreported, but it can be guessed that those we know of form only a fraction of those that have been witnessed. I can attest to this from my own experience of investigating UFO sightings. Often a witness will report an event many years after it had occurred, with the comment, 'I didn't know who to tell it to.' One can judge that a significant number of encounters have taken place where the only recipients of the details are a few friends and relations and the events do not find their way into the literature on the subject.

So can we be sure that the incidents investigated and/or written about are representative of the phenomena? Again, it seems impossible to be sure but, for example, given the number of encounters discussed by Dr McCue, one can sense that a broad pattern is established, and that whilst more examples are always of interest and may fill in gaps in our perception of the phenomena, they would not disrupt the overall parameters.

As Dr McCue suggests, there's surely a case for believing that particular stretches of road host more strange incidents than others. One may have differing views as to the manner in which that comes about. Are there actually more incidents, or simply more reports of incidents if a stretch of road earns a haunted reputation? But then again, how does a road develop a haunted reputation? Common sense would indicate that 'something' is taking place on a road, which witnesses feel they cannot explain in a straightforward way. Dr McCue, in *Paranormal Encounters on Britain's Roads: Phantom Figures, UFOs and Missing Time*, has provided a range of ideas and examples of strange incidents, allowing the reader to come to his or her own conclusion. It's a fascinating contribution to a long-standing debate and one which I'm sure will continue for many years to come!

Ron Halliday, Bridge of Allan
January 2018

PREFACE

This book is intended for general readers and for people with a special interest in paranormal and UFO matters. It aims at presenting case material and theories in a clear, objective and open-minded way. I regard myself as a cautious believer in the reality of paranormal phenomena, but I don't hold fast to any particular theory. In other words, I'm convinced that strange things happen, but I'm by no means certain *how* and *why* they occur.

Many of us spend a lot of time on roads. I recall, from my childhood, the liberating feeling that I had from acquiring a bicycle, since it enabled me to travel much further than I could walk. Years later, motorbikes gave me a renewed sense of freedom, and a romantic thrill never quite matched by driving a car. Travel on roads can be enchanting, particularly in scenic areas, such as the Scottish Highlands, the Lake District and Snowdonia. But, of course, road travel carries dangers, and tragic accidents and crime are all too common.

The literature on paranormal and UFO experiences is replete with accounts of road users encountering strange phenomena. Such incidents can leave people surprised, bewildered or traumatised. But leaving aside certain UFO close encounters, there are usually no adverse, long-term physical effects. There's a commonality about many of the reports, with certain features cropping up time and again. To me, this suggests that many of the accounts are genuine. But hard-line sceptics might claim that the commonality arises from hoaxers inventing tales in line with stories already in circulation. Certainly, it's sensible to be wary about the possibility of deliberate or accidental misreporting. Indeed, in some of the cases that I mention, different sources have given conflicting accounts.

I've referenced most of my sources in the endnotes for each chapter. In citing books in the endnotes, I've given just the main title and omitted the year of publication and details of the publisher. But this information is provided in the Bibliography, which lists, alphabetically, by author, all the print sources that I've cited.

By the time this book is published, some of the Internet items cited in it may no longer be accessible via the addresses given. But by using a search engine such as Google, it may be possible to find them elsewhere on the Internet.

Where publications give just one forename in respect of an author, I've cited it in the relevant endnote (e.g. *Budd* Hopkins). But where multiple forenames or initials have been used, I've opted for brevity and used initials (e.g. *G.L.* Playfair). However, with regard to the Bibliography, I've used initials only.

Except where indicated, I've used real names in referring to witnesses with whom I've had personal contact. With regard to the names cited by other authors, the situation isn't so clear, since writers don't always say when they're using pseudonyms. But where I'm aware that pseudonyms have been used, I've indicated that. I haven't changed any place names, and hopefully that's also the case with the places mentioned by the authors I've cited.

In quoting people, I've occasionally edited the material very slightly for presentational purposes, but I haven't changed the substantive content.

The majority of the photographs appearing in this book were taken by me. In the four instances where that wasn't the case, I've included the name of the photographer in the relevant caption.

Regarding the index, I haven't included the names of *all* the witnesses mentioned throughout the book, since some of the cases are little known and, in many instances, the people referred to may have been given pseudonyms.

FUNDAMENTALS

The scientific investigation of paranormal phenomena is called *psychical research*, and the manifestations themselves, where deemed genuine, are often referred to as *psi phenomena* or simply *psi*. In this chapter, I'll discuss some basic concepts and theories from psychical research, to help make sense of the case material that's the main focus of the book. Since many road users have UFO experiences, I'll also discuss concepts and theories pertaining to the UFO topic. The study of UFO phenomena isn't traditionally regarded as being within the domain of psychical research, but there's a considerable overlap, since many UFO experiences have paranormal features.

In passing, it's worth noting that the term *parapsychology* is sometimes employed as a synonym of psychical research. However, in the UK, at least, it tends to be used in a narrower sense, to refer to experimental psi research carried out in laboratory-type settings. In terms of this distinction, all parapsychologists are psychical researchers, but not all psychical researchers are parapsychologists. For example, investigators who focus on apparitions, hauntings and poltergeist cases could be described as psychical researchers; but if they don't carry out laboratory-type research, they might not be regarded as parapsychologists.

EXTRASENSORY PERCEPTION (ESP)

Extrasensory perception (ESP) is the acquisition of information by non-sensory (i.e. paranormal) means. Judging from spontaneous cases, it often occurs automatically – that is, without any conscious intention on the part of those involved. The information might express itself in consciousness via a thought, feeling, vision or dream. Imagine the following (hypothetical) scenario:

> Megan drops off her 4-year-old son, David, at a nursery and then goes to her place of work, the local library. Shortly before the library opens to the public, she has an ESP experience that induces her to return, urgently, to the nursery, where she discovers that her son has had a nasty accident and is asking for her.

In this situation, Megan's ESP experience could take the form of a sudden feeling of uneasiness and her having an urge to go to her son immediately. Alternatively, a fleeting apparition of David might appear before her, making her feel that something's badly wrong and that she needs to get to him without delay. Later, she might discover that the apparition appeared at the very time of his accident. Another possibility (if the ESP is of a *precognitive* type – see below) is that Megan will dream about the accident in advance. If so, it might prompt her to take action to prevent the accident from occurring.

Various types of ESP can be distinguished, at least in theory: *telepathy*, *clairvoyance*, *precognition* and *retrocognition*.

Telepathy

Telepathy means direct mind-to-mind communication. For example, someone might sense feelings, or pick up information, from a distant friend or relative, or might mentally transmit an image to that person. On occasions, the communication might involve more than just two individuals. Telepathic interaction may occur among animals, and there's evidence suggesting that telepathy can occur between people and their pets.[1] Norris McWhirter, an author and editor, had what may have been a telepathic experience in 1975. He was at home and suddenly slumped into a chair. He recovered a few minutes later, but the police then rang to say that his twin brother, Ross, who lived 6 miles away, had been shot dead.[2]

It might be wrong to think of telepathy as some sort of mental radio in which thoughts, images or feelings are transmitted across space. It may be that individual human beings and other sentient animals are fundamentally part of one collective mind, and that our sense of individuality is illusory. If so, a person's thoughts, feelings or impressions may be potentially available to everyone else. The fact that we're not constantly aware of one another's thoughts and feelings could be because some sort of filtering normally operates.

Clairvoyance

The word *clairvoyance* comes from French words meaning 'clear seeing'. Psychical researchers use it to refer to a form of ESP in which someone acquires information about a physical situation elsewhere, but without using the physical senses or telepathy. Imagine, for instance, a computerised experiment in which: (1) Randomly selected letters of the alphabet are displayed, one at a time, on a screen in an empty room while a subject – let's call her Julie – is located elsewhere and tries to discern what they are; (2) Julie registers her guesses by pressing the appropriate keys on a computer keyboard; (3) A computer records the number of correct guesses, *but without anyone ever knowing (by any normal means) what letter was displayed on the screen at any given point* (thereby excluding telepathy). Now, if Julie scores significantly above (or below) what would be expected by chance, we might infer that she has displayed clairvoyance (or that someone else has obtained the information by clairvoyance and has conveyed it to Julie telepathically). However, another possibility would be that, via psychokinesis (a 'mind over matter' effect), Julie has influenced the selection of target letters or has made the computer record an incorrect number of supposedly correct guesses.

At first sight, clairvoyance seems very different from telepathy, since it entails direct awareness of physical events. However, if the physical world is ultimately a construction of the collective mind of humans and other sentient creatures – a sort of sustained hallucination – knowledge of every aspect of it may be known to the collective mind. Accordingly, there may be no fundamental difference between telepathy and clairvoyance, since both may entail becoming aware of what the collective mind already knows.

Precognition

Imagine another experiment. Every 10 seconds, Julie guesses the identity of a letter of the alphabet that will be randomly selected by a computer *after* she has made her guess. If she's capable of *precognition* (acquiring information, paranormally, about the future), she may score significantly above (or below) what would be expected by chance. Again, though, if the results significantly differ from chance expectation, another possibility is that psychokinesis (PK) has come into play, enabling Julie – presumably unconsciously – to influence the selection of target letters or make the computer record an incorrect number of supposedly correct guesses.

Jenny Randles mentions a possible instance of precognition involving a friend of hers. The friend was driving on the M62 motorway near Warrington, Cheshire, and, for no apparent conscious reason, swerved into the fast lane. Seconds later, a truck that had been ahead of her shed its load, which bounced across the carriageway where Randles' friend would have been if she hadn't veered into the fast lane.[3]

Precognition raises intriguing theoretical questions. If events can be foreseen, does the future in some sense already exist, and is our sense of free will illusory? Or could it be that precognitive experiences are essentially predictions about the future, based on *current* information that's gleaned, unconsciously, by telepathy or clairvoyance? Another possibility is that the information about what's going to happen in the future comes from an omniscient higher intelligence.

Retrocognition

There are accounts of people temporarily experiencing their surroundings as if they'd gone back in time. Psychical researchers refer to this as *retrocognition*, although such incidents are better known as *time-slips*. The late Andrew MacKenzie discusses an incident from 1957 in which three youths possibly saw a Suffolk village (Kersey) as it had been centuries before. The main informant, William Laing, first contacted MacKenzie about the incident in 1988. Michael Crowley, one of the other witnesses, didn't remember the occasion clearly, but provided some corroboration of Laing's recollections. However, it seems that the third person, Ray Baker, recalled little or nothing of the village.[4]

A correspondent informed me about a puzzling incident from the summer of 1939. It may have been a time-slip. She and her future husband were in the habit of going for evening walks through the Camperdown Estate near Dundee. On the occasion in question, they entered a clearing in a wooded area and saw a summer house made of logs, with a paved path leading up to it. The next evening, they went the same way. But much to their dismay, they couldn't find the summer house. My informant wrote: 'Search as we did do, we never, ever found [it]. For ages after that we looked and looked [...]. But never did we find it.' Was the summer house there all the time, in a woodland clearing that the couple repeatedly failed to relocate? Or could their experience have been a shared hallucination? If so, what produced it, and did the hallucination represent a scene that actually existed at some point in the past? Or did the couple literally go back in time for a short period? We shall probably never know.

Distinguishing between different types of ESP

When ESP occurs outside controlled laboratory settings, it will generally be impossible to know whether it's of a telepathic, clairvoyant or precognitive nature. Take, for example, the aforementioned incident involving Norris McWhirter. Subconsciously, he may have been clairvoyantly monitoring his brother's physical circumstances. The analogy of a radar installation monitoring a section of airspace comes to mind. If so, there may have been no mind-to-mind communication (telepathy) between the twins. Precognition is another possibility: McWhirter's mind may have reached into the future and anticipated that he was about to receive bad news about his brother. However, as explained above, in terms of a theory involving a collective mind, there may be no fundamental difference between telepathy and clairvoyance; and precognition could, perhaps, be explained in terms of unconscious prediction based on telepathically or clairvoyantly acquired information, or of information being fed to people by a higher intelligence.

In the hypothetical case of Megan and David, one of the scenarios involved the mother seeing an apparition of her son and later discovering that he'd had an accident at that very time. In the parlance of psychical researchers, this would be described as a *crisis apparition* case, and it's not hard to find reports of seemingly real incidents of that type.[5]

It would be beyond the scope of this book to go into detail about laboratory-based experimental psi research, but Dean Radin, a parapsychologist based in the USA, provides a readable account of it in his book *Entangled Minds*. Suffice it to say that there appears to be considerable evidence for psi from such studies.

PARANORMAL PHYSICAL EFFECTS

Psychical researchers have endeavoured to elicit psychokinetic ('mind over matter') effects experimentally. For example, in 1972, some members of the Toronto Society for Psychical Research set about trying to do this. They created an identity for a fictitious spirit communicator (a seventeenth-century aristocratic Englishman, whom they named 'Philip'). This was to help circumvent 'ownership resistance', a hypothesised reluctance that people might have to identifying themselves as the source of paranormal activity. They met frequently over an extended period and eventually elicited physical phenomena, such as raps and large movements of a table. But they didn't seriously believe that a disembodied spirit was responsible.[6]

Remarkable manifestations have allegedly occurred in the presence of physical mediums. For example, the Scottish-born medium Daniel Dunglas Home (1833–86) reportedly produced a wide range of phenomena, such as levitation of his own body, levitation of furniture, materialisations, luminous appearances and percussive sounds.

Spontaneous episodes of disruptive physical activity of a paranormal kind are known as *poltergeist* outbreaks, although some writers prefer the term *recurrent spontaneous psychokinesis* (RSPK). One of the best-known British cases from recent decades involved a mother and her four children occupying a council house in Enfield, on the northern fringe of London. Phenomena such as object movements, disturbance of bedclothes, the appearance of pools of water, and human levitation were reported. The manifestations occurred between August 1977 and the autumn of 1978, with a brief recurrence sometime later.[7] But given that poltergeist episodes are generally quite brief, the Enfield case wasn't entirely typical.

Poltergeist phenomena are often attributed to a living agent, a 'poltergeist focus', if such a person can be identified, which isn't always the case. It's often assumed that the manifestations reflect psychological tension or changes associated with puberty, and that they are produced unconsciously by the focal person. But they may be produced consciously in some instances. A seventeenth-century poltergeist case in Wiltshire, England, in what's now known as North Tidworth, seemed to involve conscious agency on the part of a living person named William Drury, although he didn't appear to have been on the scene when the manifestations occurred. The case could, perhaps, be construed as one of malicious witchcraft.[8]

The notion that poltergeist phenomena are generated by living people hasn't gone unchallenged. Some people argue that discarnate spirits may be involved. Another possibility is that some sort of tricksterish, higher intelligence plays a role. (In referring to a *higher* intelligence, I mean one that's more resourceful than we are. I don't mean to imply that it's necessarily morally superior.)

APPARITIONS AND HAUNTINGS

Apparitional experiences are often one-off events. The term 'haunting' or 'haunt' is applied to cases featuring *recurrent* manifestations, of an apparently paranormal nature, that seem to be linked with particular places rather than specific people. Although clear-cut physical phenomena are reported in many haunt cases, the manifestations are sometimes wholly, or predominantly, of a sensory character (sights, sounds, tactile impressions, etc.). Hauntings vary in duration, some being very long-running.

Theories about apparitions

Transient materialisations

Apparitional figures have sometimes been caught on film.[9] If a supposed photograph of a ghostly figure is deemed to be genuine (i.e. not the result of deliberate fakery or a trick of the light), there would appear to be two possibilities: a mysterious force affected the camera, making it record something not present; or some sort of transient materialisation occurred. Similarly, a supposed recording of ghostly sounds could be the result of a mysterious force affecting the recording apparatus; or it could be an actual recording of physical sound.

If apparitions and ghostly sounds have a degree of physical reality, it's not surprising that they're often perceived collectively (i.e. by two or more people at the same time). However, there are also cases in which this *doesn't* happen – where, for example, not everyone present sees a phantom figure. Of course, such instances don't accord well with the notion that apparitions have a physical aspect.

Myers' theory

Frederic Myers (1843–1901) was one of the founders of the Society for Psychical Research. He suggested that in some apparitional cases, an aspect of the agent (the person whose apparition is seen) might actually be present in the space where a phantom figure is discerned or where a ghostly sound is heard. However, it's not clear how those present would 'see' or 'hear' such a presence. Myers suggested that an unknown form of supernormal perception, not necessarily involving the normal senses, comes into play.[10]

Telepathically engendered hallucinations

Some psychical researchers – for example, the late George Tyrrell (1879–1952) – have suggested that apparitions are hallucinations engendered by telepathy. Imagine, for example, that a man has a fatal road accident at midday and that his wife, at home some miles away, has a fleeting vision of him at that time. In terms of a telepathy-based theory, it might be conjectured that the husband thought of his wife at the time of the accident, earnestly wishing that he could be with her, and that, via an unconscious telepathic process, this resulted in her hallucinating him.

As noted, apparitions are often perceived collectively. For example, if a driver sees a phantom figure on the road ahead, passengers in the car might also see it. This isn't easy to explain in terms of a telepathy-based theory. Tyrrell argued that the explanation 'lies [...] in the fact that spectators, by their physical presence, become *relevant* to the theme of the apparitional idea-pattern and, because relevant, are drawn into it' (emphasis as in the original).[11] This isn't very clear, but the essential idea, from the perspective of Tyrrell's theory, is that *the apparitional process tends to mimic ordinary perception.* If a wife were looking at her husband in their living room, any visitor present would be expected to see him as well. Therefore, if the wife sees an apparition of her husband, a visitor might be drawn in (via telepathy) and see it as well, because that's what would happen if the husband were physically present.

Tyrrell argued that the agents behind apparitional events could be either living people or the surviving selves of deceased persons. Discussing a haunting in Cheltenham, he stated that he could see no plausible agent other than the surviving self or personality of a deceased woman whose appearance and habits the apparition reproduced.[12] He suggested that the 'ghostly theme' in such a case is one of 'brooding reminiscence', with the 'ghostly drama' being 'that of the agent's figure performing long familiar actions in a familiar place' (p. 143). But regarding another case with haunt-type phenomena, he suggested that the agent was a living person, a cook, whose departure from the afflicted household was followed by a cessation of the phenomena. Noting that, even in the Cheltenham case, 'unintelligent noises developed during its peak period', Tyrrell suggested that some hauntings may be complex, 'being partly the reminiscent type of ghost of a deceased person and partly the poltergeistic type originated by some living person on the spot'; and he speculated that, 'Possibly the one type stimulates the other in some way' (p. 145).

I don't find these ideas very lucid. However, if Tyrrell was correct in suggesting that brooding reminiscence by the spirit of a dead person can instigate ghostly phenomena in a place that he or she once frequented, maybe living people can sometimes do the same, by repeatedly thinking of certain places. Indeed, there have been reports of 'ghosts of the living'. For example, a woman was reportedly seen in a Dr E.'s house in October 1886 and then again on two occasions several months later. In the summer of 1888, Dr E.'s son returned to England from Australia, accompanied by his wife, whom he'd met on his travels. Having recently been ill, she was gaunt when she met the family, and she wasn't immediately linked with the former ghost. But several days later, when she appeared for dinner in good health, wearing a brown dress with a lace collar, she was recognised by a servant and a guest who had previously seen the apparition. During casual conversation, she remarked that during her illness in 1886 she'd often tried to picture what the house of her new relatives looked like.[13]

If I've understood Tyrrell's theory correctly, it implies that in the case of haunting apparitions, the manifestations serve no real purpose and the agent will probably be unaware that he or she is causing people to experience hallucinations in the haunted location. But a problem with the theory is that it doesn't account for the physical phenomena that are frequently reported in cases of haunting (e.g. displacement of objects, opening of doors and disturbance of bedclothes). Furthermore, I find it hard to imagine how 'brooding reminiscence' by a former occupant of a house could establish telepathic links with subsequent occupants of the property (whom the earlier occupant might never have known), causing them to experience hallucinations.

Tyrrell's book is mainly about human apparitions. However, there are many reports of non-human apparitions, including, for example, phantom animals, phantom vehicles, fairies, and even phantom buildings. Some UFO sightings may also be apparitional events. In terms of a telepathic theory such as Tyrrell's, the agency behind such manifestations seems far from clear.

The traditional spiritualist stance

Spiritualists contend that many apparitions are discarnate spirits (or representations of spirits) who have become 'stuck' in crossing to the afterlife. This notion also predominates in fictional ghost stories and films, and seems to be accepted, rather uncritically, by many self-styled 'ghost hunters' and 'paranormal investigators'.

True Hauntings: Spirits with a Purpose, a book by the late Hazel Denning, exemplifies the spiritualist approach. One of the cases that Denning mentions involved a young man and his wife who had heard knockings and footsteps in their home, with the wife also seeing an apparition of a woman whose description seemed to fit her husband's recently deceased mother. Denning visited the couple with a psychically gifted associate, Gertrude, who allegedly contacted the deceased mother. The latter indicated that she was very unhappy about being 'earthbound'. Her bereaved son had thought of her so often, and with so much grief, that 'the energy' (Denning's words) had held her to him. She'd tried very hard to demonstrate that she was still a living spirit. Two weeks after Gertrude's mediation, Denning contacted the couple again, and was informed that there'd been no further manifestations. Unfortunately, though, we're not told *how* the deceased mother produced the phenomena, and it's not clear whether the apparition of her was hallucinatory or was in some sense objective.[14]

Of course, it may be that Denning's psychic colleague, Gertrude, really did contact the spirit of the young man's mother. Another possibility is that the phenomena were orchestrated by a tricksterish intelligence that simply pretended to be the deceased mother. Alternatively, the 'spirit' could have been a figment of Gertrude's imagination; but by convincing the bereaved son that his mother was alive in the spirit world, she may have resolved psychological factors that were somehow generating the phenomena.

However, it's hard to believe that human apparitions are literally spirits, because they generally appear clothed and they sometimes display other accoutrements, such as weapons. Even the notion that they're *representations* of spirits is questionable. Take, for example, a case from the nineteenth century – the haunting of the mill house at Willington Quay, near Wallsend, in the north-east of England. In addition to frequent auditory phenomena, there were sightings of *different types* of apparition, such as that of a white and transparent female figure, of a boy with a drab hat, and of a monkey! Now, if these figures are deemed to have been representations of earthbound spirits, we have to ask how it was that such a variety of them became earthbound at that one particular site.[15]

Played-back recordings

In her book, Hazel Denning suggested that some cases, which she called *pseudo-hauntings*, don't entail the active intervention of spirit entities, but rather an 'energy form created by traumatic events [that] seems to be charged with a powerful energy that continues to exist […] for a considerable length of time' (p. 128). Others have expressed similar ideas. From this perspective, seeing or hearing ghostly manifestations can be likened to watching or hearing the playback of a video recording of something from the past. For example, if motorists see Roman soldiers from centuries ago marching beside the M6 motorway, the vision could be construed as the 'playback' of some sort of recording from a time when the Romans were in that area.

Jenny Randles' book *Supernatural Pennines* mentions the case of Nellie, a woman living in an isolated cottage on the moors outside Todmorden, West Yorkshire. (Since Todmorden is near the border of West Yorkshire and Lancashire, the cottage itself may have been in either area – Randles doesn't say.) Nellie had experienced many strange electrical problems in her home; and, on several occasions, she had heard her son's motorcycle coming up the hillside, followed by the sound of its being parked in the yard and then the door opening. However, those were sounds from a bygone time, since her son no longer visited the cottage on a motorbike.[16] Randles notes that the cottage was built of a millstone rich in quartz crystals, and she speculates that it acted like a video recorder, capturing sounds from the past. But she makes no mention of anyone other than Nellie hearing the supposed auditory replay. It's possible, therefore, that the sounds were hallucinatory.

Environmental factors

Environmental factors, such as magnetic fields, seismic activity and low frequency sound, are thought by some researchers to play a role in ghostly manifestations and UFO phenomena. For example, Michael Persinger and Stanley Koren mention the case of a 17-year-old high school student who was reporting experiences such as visions, vibration of her bed, and hearing footsteps and humming. She'd incurred some brain trauma as a young child, which may have been a predisposing factor. However, the authors note that she'd been sleeping with an electric clock near her head, and that it emitted a pulsed magnetic field. Her negative subjective experiences ceased when she started sleeping in an area where the ambient magnetic fields were less than 1 milligauss. [17] (I presume that the authors are referring here to man-made fields, and disregarding the background geomagnetic field.) However, with most of the cases discussed in this book, I doubt whether unusual magnetic fields and suchlike can provide a credible explanation of the witnesses' experiences. They were generally walking on, or driving along, roads at the time. Therefore, any exposure to highly localised energy fields (e.g. from power lines) should have been brief.

False memories

The expression 'false memory syndrome' has been applied to cases in which methods such as hypnosis have been used to try and elicit recollections of possible trauma, and where leading questions and suggestion have had the unfortunate effect of instilling false memories in people (e.g. historically untrue recollections of having been sexually abused). However, in the present context, I mean something rather different: the possibility that, on occasions, *a mysterious, paranormal force* is able to edit people's memories. The following is a hypothetical example:

> Joe Bloggs calls at a police station and reports that 25 minutes previously he was driving along a country lane when a female figure ran out in front of his car and was knocked down. He explains that despite stopping and searching under the car, and on both sides of the road, he was unable to find her body. The police visit the scene with Joe and notice skid marks. But they, too, are unable to find an accident victim. Furthermore, they notice that Joe's car shows no sign of damage.

Now, of course, what Joe has told the police is based on his *recall* of what happened. But what if a false memory had somehow been instilled? Imagine, for instance, that just before the supposed collision, he'd been thinking about a forthcoming holiday, and then a *false*, but subjectively compelling, memory of having collided with a female pedestrian had been inserted into his mind. Believing, on the basis of this false memory, that he'd just run over someone, it would, of course, be entirely natural and appropriate for him to stop and search for the victim, and his recollection of that part of the proceedings could well be entirely accurate.

This notion of memory tampering may sound far-fetched, but when it comes to UFO-related experiences, there are many instances in which people have reported mysterious memory blanks, or what's popularly called 'missing time'. Examples will be given in later chapters.

THE UFO PHENOMENON

The abbreviation 'UFO' stands for *unidentified flying object*, and is widely applied to all sorts of unknown or anomalous aerial phenomena, ranging from sightings of structured craft to small balls of light. As such, *UFO* is a question-begging term, since it's not always clear whether *objects* as such are responsible for the sightings. Another problem is that some people automatically equate UFOs with alien spaceships, although that's just one of many possible interpretations. Objects on the ground that could be construed as landed aerial craft of unidentified origin are also referred to as UFOs. It's also worth noting that UFOs are sometimes seen to enter, or emerge from, the sea or other bodies of water, and that mysterious underwater objects have reportedly been detected by equipment. On investigation, many UFOs lose their unidentified status. For example, mysterious lights in the sky might turn out to be space debris burning up on re-entry to the atmosphere, or balloons, bright planets, Chinese lanterns or other natural or man-made objects.

I shall use the singular form, 'UFO phenomenon', to refer to the general subject of UFOs. As such, the expression equates to 'the UFO enigma' or 'the UFO problem'. I'll use the plural form, 'UFO phenomena', to refer to the manifestations themselves. In terms of this distinction, one could say that someone became interested in *the UFO phenomenon* after witnessing *UFO phenomena*.

The alien abduction controversy

After UFO sightings, witnesses are sometimes unable to account for periods of time. They might be haunted by vague feelings, flashbacks and partial recollections. They might discover marks or scars that they hadn't previously noticed, or they might become aware of small foreign objects ('implants') within their bodies. Over time, or with the aid of hypnotic regression, they might recall abduction scenarios involving otherworldly entities. Accounts often feature medical examinations and reproductive procedures. Indeed, it has been suggested that aliens are systematically engaged in creating human–alien hybrids, and are using human female abductees as incubators. For many people, abduction seems to be a recurrent experience, and is often a source of considerable distress. Furthermore, there are cases in which different generations within a family have seemingly been targeted. Thus, a woman with a history of abduction experiences might be dismayed to discover that her daughter is going through a similar ordeal.

Missing Time, a book by the late Budd Hopkins, cited UFO-related abduction experiences recalled under hypnosis, and helped to raise awareness of the abduction phenomenon. But there had been earlier reports of abductions, and there have been stories in folklore about fairies abducting people. However, the use of hypnosis in abduction research is controversial, because of the possibility of suggestion and imagination creating false or distorted memories. Carol Rainey, an ex-wife of Hopkins, has criticised the way that he and a colleague handled cases.[18] She claims, for instance, that he allowed himself to be duped by hoaxers. Hopkins wrote a rejoinder.[19]

Author Albert Budden contends that electric and magnetic fields can induce suitably sensitised people to experience hallucinations with a ghostly or UFO theme. One of the cases he cites is from Australia and concerns a woman called Maureen Puddy, who had a history of anomalous experiences. In February 1973, she undertook a fairly long car journey to meet UFO researchers Judith Magee and Paul Norman. During the journey, she had a brief vision of a 'spaceman' in her car. Magee and Norman were waiting for her when she arrived. When Magee touched the bodywork of Puddy's car, she (Magee) experienced a strong electric shock, presumably meaning that a static electric charge had discharged itself through her. (Budden quotes from an anonymous source that claims that unexpectedly high magnetic fields were detected in Puddy's car, in the vicinity of the front seats.) Magee and Norman sat with Puddy in her car, to conduct the interview. As she was telling the investigators about seeing the spaceman, she broke off and indicated that she was seeing him again. However, Magee and Norman saw nothing. Puddy said that the figure had walked towards the car and was standing in front of it. Norman got out and walked to the front of the car, after which Puddy explained that the spaceman had moved back to let him pass. Then, she apparently saw the figure beckoning to her, after which it appeared to melt away into some bushes. Puddy then screamed that she was being abducted, and she gave details of the interior of a flying saucer in which she found herself. Eventually, she returned to her normal state.[20]

Of course, the Puddy case suggests that at least some abduction experiences are purely subjective events. However, even if they have no objective, physical reality, it's possible that an external intelligence induces people to have such experiences. Furthermore, some cases involve more than one person and aren't easily accounted for in terms of fantasy-proneness. Examples will be given in a later chapter.

Theories

Strictly speaking, a theory is a formal, systematically elaborated and internally consistent set of propositions advanced to explain something, whereas a hypothesis (by definition, something less than a thesis) is just one explanatory proposal. In this sense, a theory (an overarching set of ideas or principles) might generate a number of specific (and hopefully testable) hypotheses. But in the domain of ufology, people tend to use 'theory' and 'hypothesis' interchangeably. For instance, the notion that UFO phenomena and supposedly paranormal events can be accounted for in terms of social and psychological factors (cultural beliefs, the influence of science fiction, misperception, hoaxing, illusions, fantasy, etc.) is referred to as the 'psychosocial *hypothesis*', although it would probably be more accurate to describe it as a theory. Similarly, the notion that some UFOs are spacecraft, piloted or controlled by extraterrestrial beings, is often referred to as the 'extraterrestrial *hypothesis*', although it might be more accurate to describe it as a theory.

The psychosocial hypothesis
As noted, advocates of the psychosocial hypothesis (PSH) favour prosaic (non-paranormal) explanations of anomalous experiences. Imagine, for instance, that someone in a supposedly haunted house reports hearing ghostly footsteps. From the perspective of the PSH, this might be attributed to suggestion and misinterpretation of normal noises caused, for example, by creaking floorboards or the vagaries of the plumbing system. Similarly, an illusion known as the *autokinetic effect* could lead people to interpret a

fixed point of light in the night sky, such as a star, as a UFO. The illusion occurs when a stationary source of light is set against a dark or featureless background with no reference point. The light appears to move about, but that's a normal perceptual effect.

Advocates of the PSH contend that people interpret anomalous experiences in terms of prevailing cultural beliefs. For example, when a belief in fairies was widespread, experiences involving diminutive humanoid figures would have been interpreted as fairy sightings, whereas nowadays such figures might be regarded as extraterrestrial aliens. PSH proponents have drawn attention to parallels between UFO experiences and science fiction. Of course, with some people, science fiction might well foster a fascination with UFOs and ideas of alien visitation, which could result in their looking at the sky and mistaking aircraft, balloons, bright planets, etc., for alien spaceships. With particularly imaginative and suggestible individuals, cultural stereotypes influenced by science fiction might, perhaps, engender believed-in fantasies and pseudo-memories with a UFO or alien theme. Similarly, exposure to television series such as *Most Haunted* could lead people to misinterpret innocuous sounds or temperature variations as evidence that their homes are haunted by restless spirits. But if some UFO experiences are choreographed paranormal events, it wouldn't be surprising if they resembled science fiction and reflected contemporary preoccupations.

Some people seem to be especially prone to unusual experiences. Possibly, they're genuinely psychic and able to pick up impressions via ESP and affect their environment, wittingly or unwittingly, via PK. Similarly, when people report alien abduction experiences, it may be that they have indeed been abducted. Psychosocial theorists, however, might suggest that these people are simply more prone to illusions, believed-in fantasies and misperception than the rest of us. However, it's far from clear that that's necessarily the case. Peter Hough refers to various studies, including one that he conducted with the assistance of Dr Paul Rogers of the University of Central Lancashire. Among other things, they compared abductees with control subjects. But they found no significant differences between them regarding factors such as emotional intelligence, fantasy-proneness, extraversion, emotional stability and openness to experience.[21]

Some advocates of the PSH appear to believe that *all* UFO incidents would turn out to have normal explanations if only sufficient information were available. Logically, though, there's no need to take such an extreme position. No doubt many UFO cases can be satisfactorily explained, at least to some degree, in terms of psychosocial factors and/or normal physical causes. But others may well entail something paranormal or exotic.

Geophysical factors

According to the website of the British author and researcher Paul Devereux, he believes that the majority of UFO reports arise from misperception, mirages, hoaxes and psychological effects (e.g. witnesses experiencing trance states).[22] As such, he appears to be an adherent of the PSH. However, he contends that a small proportion of experiences arise from unexplained phenomena, including geophysical or meteorological manifestations that he calls *earth lights*. He depicts them as straddling the boundary between the normal and the paranormal. He contends that they're related to earthquake lights and ball lightning, although he thinks they have characteristics of their own. For example, they sometimes last longer than earthquake lights and ball lightning. He believes that they're associated with stresses and strains in the Earth's crust, but can occur in the absence of actual earthquakes, and that they have electrical and magnetic properties. He states that, 'some form of plasma is assumed'. He notes that witnesses who come close to earth lights typically report hallucinatory experiences, and that earth lights sometimes behave as if they had a rudimentary intelligence. Another observation is that they sometimes manifest illogical effects, such as being visible from one side, but not the other. Devereux infers that they may be what he calls *macro-quantal events* – 'phenomena that should only exist at the sub-atomic quantum level, but [which somehow manifest] on our larger macro-scale of experience'.

The American neuropsychologist Michael Persinger also contends that environmental factors, such as tectonic strain, can play a role in UFO experiences.

Jung's theory

Carl Gustav Jung (1875–1961) was a Swiss-born psychiatrist. For several years, he collaborated with Sigmund Freud, the founder of psychoanalysis. He then established his own school of thought, known as 'analytical psychology'. In a book, first published in English in 1959, he addressed the UFO phenomenon.[23] The book is written in rather convoluted and opaque language, and accepts that there may be an objective component to the UFO phenomenon. However, it largely treats it from a psychological perspective, in terms of visions that give expression to the supposed collective unconscious mind. The book was written during the Cold War, and it relates the 'visionary rumours', as Jung called them, to 'an *emotional tension* having its cause in a situation of collective distress or danger, or in a vital psychic need' (p. 7; emphasis as in the original). Among other things, Jung appeared to suggest that UFO sightings might involve disc-shaped or spherical objects because the mandala (Sanskrit for circle) is a symbol of totality or order, and represents a 'protective' circle (p. 15)! However, it should be noted that many UFOs are *not* disc-shaped or spherical. Indeed, nowadays, many of them seem to be triangular. At any rate, since I regard Jung's treatment of this subject as lacking clarity and coherence, I shan't dwell on it further.

The extraterrestrial hypothesis

The extraterrestrial hypothesis (ETH) is the notion that some UFOs are piloted or remotely controlled craft operated by intelligent beings from elsewhere in the universe. Various motives have been ascribed to the presumed visitors, including: (1) Scientific curiosity about our planet and the life forms that inhabit it; (2) The acquisition of minerals or other materials needed by the visitors; (3) Monitoring of human activity that could conflict with the interests of the space visitors; (4) Preparation for a takeover of Earth in the light of difficulties that the aliens might be experiencing on their home planet(s). (This preparation could include cross-breeding with humans, to incorporate some of our genetic material, to help the aliens adapt to conditions on Earth.) Of course, these possible motives aren't mutually exclusive. However, there are problems for the ETH. For example, UFOs appear in a bewildering array of shapes and sizes, often displaying an apparitional and evanescent character that isn't in keeping with their being solid spaceships with an enduring existence.

Jacques Vallee is a French-born scientist, now based in the USA. He has written extensively about the UFO phenomenon, which he regards as genuinely anomalous. He started out favouring the ETH, but soon abandoned it. An appendix to his book *Revelations* contains a presentation (given at a conference in 1989) entitled 'Five arguments against the extraterrestrial origin of unidentified flying objects'.

Vallee's first argument concerns the number of 'close encounter' experiences, which, it seems, run into the thousands, or perhaps very many thousands. He contends that such a large number exceeds what one would expect if space explorers were analysing a planet's soil or taking biological samples to produce a complete map. But if there's a substantial resident population of extraterrestrial beings here on Earth – a possibility thatVallee's presentation doesn't address – there could be numerous close encounters without requiring a commensurate number of spaceflights from orbiting 'mother ships' or distant planets.Vallee's fourth argument is similar to the first. It concerns the long history of UFO or UFO-like phenomena, which he views as inconsistent with the notion that extraterrestrials are carrying out a survey of our planet.Vallee's second argument is related to the anatomy of the reported aliens. He notes that the vast majority of them have characteristics (two arms, two legs, a head, etc.) suggesting a genetic constitution close to ours. He contends that this would be unlikely if they had evolved independently on another planet. He raises the possibility that genetic manipulation has been employed to create ET beings that can interact with us. But if that's the case, he asks, why aren't they biologically indistinguishable from us? Arguably, though, if there are aliens who can manipulate their genetic material, there might be distinct advantages for them (in terms of intelligence, memory, longevity, etc.) in retaining some features that are different from those of the human race.The third ofVallee's arguments concerns the claim, by some ufologists, that the growing number of abduction reports supports the ETH.Vallee contends that a team of ET scientists, equipped with the UFO technology commonly reported, would be in an excellent position to take control of blood banks, sperm banks or collections of embryos at major hospitals and research centres, obviating the need to subject humans to the disturbing experiences that feature in alien abduction reports. However, this presupposes that the aliens would have some sympathy or compassion towards humans, which might not be the case.Vallee's fifth argument is that UFOs apparently have the ability to manipulate space and time, which – he contends – suggests radically different and richer alternatives to the ETH.

Time travel
A rather speculative hypothesis is that some UFOs are time machines from our future.This notion gets around one of the problems faced by the ETH: the fact that UFO occupants often resemble ourselves, and seem fairly well adapted to terrestrial conditions, which would perhaps be unlikely if they had evolved in a completely different solar system. However, so far as I'm aware, in terms of scientific knowledge, time travel is at best a theoretical possibility. Furthermore, the notion of time travel throws up awkward questions concerning causality (cause and effect). If time travellers from the

future went back to the past, they would have to be careful not to make changes that could preclude their future existence. For example, if I went back to the past and persuaded my newly married parents not to have any children, I'd presumably not be here writing this book!

Alternative realities

Another speculative notion is that exotic UFOs (i.e. those that aren't simply unidentified natural phenomena, misperceived terrestrial aircraft, etc.) come from 'another dimension' or what might be described as an alternative or parallel reality. This might help to explain the fact that UFOs, or supposed aliens, sometimes appear and disappear suddenly and mysteriously. Notions about 'many worlds' or 'parallel universes' have been discussed by theoretical physicists – for example, by David Deutsch[24] and Fred Alan Wolf[25] – and have appeared in science fiction. But sharing a world or reality is different from living in a completely separate one. Any distinction between supposedly alternative worlds or realities becomes a bit blurred if beings can go back and forth between them.

'Psychic internets'

Could it be that people's minds sometimes interact at a subconscious level and generate paranormal phenomena? If so, could this be in response to a collective wish for there to be evidence of UFOs, ghosts, life after death, etc.? Because the notion of a network of interacting minds conjures up an image of computers linked to one another via the Internet, I'll call this the *psychic internet theory*. However, since I've drawn on existing ideas (particularly Tyrrell's theory of apparitions), I can't claim that this theory is wholly original. To the extent that the effects of psychic internets are mediated by telepathy (which doesn't seem to be constrained by physical distance), the people who unconsciously instigate the phenomena wouldn't need to be in close physical proximity to one another. Indeed, maybe they wouldn't even need to know one another, although personal acquaintanceship might facilitate the subconscious networking.

As well as being able to produce apparitions in the way that Tyrrell suggested, a psychic internet might be capable of eliciting psychokinetic effects (object movements, transient materialisations, etc.). But that might require the presence, in the vicinity, of someone who is linked with the psychic internet and who has the capacity to generate psychokinetic phenomena. So far as paranormal hallucinatory phenomena are concerned, the witnesses themselves would be linked to a psychic internet, although perhaps only briefly. However, in the case of someone living in a haunted location and experiencing recurrent phenomena over a lengthy period, his or her unwitting connection with a psychic internet could be protracted.

If they exist, psychic internets may function as complex mechanisms rather than as 'higher minds', and some of their 'outputs' could be purposeless, mischievous or even malign. If they're able to fabricate evidence of extraterrestrial visitation, it might be impossible to tell whether any UFOs have an exotic origin. Similarly, if they're able to fabricate communications from the dead, it might be impossible to obtain incontrovertible evidence of post-mortem survival.

The 'size' of a psychic internet (the number of people linked together by it) could change over time. So, too, might the pattern of links among those involved. Consequently, psychic internets could have a changeable and unpredictable character. Generally, though, large psychic internets might be expected to be more powerful than smaller ones.

If somewhere acquired a reputation for being a UFO hot spot or for being haunted, it's conceivable that a collective desire to hear of further phenomena could create psychic internets that would be capable of engendering further manifestations at the site. Similarly, it's conceivable that if a spurious case received sufficient publicity, but without people realising that it was spurious, psychic internets could then start to produce genuine manifestations! Furthermore, it's possible that psychic internets are responsible for other types of anomalous phenomena, including some crop formations and sightings of out-of-place animals. People who investigate UFO incidents and paranormal phenomena might themselves become involved in psychic internets, thereby unwittingly affecting the nature or occurrence of the phenomena under study.

Psychic internets could persist despite a turnover of participants. The analogy of a political party comes to mind: the original founders might leave or die, but with new members joining, the organisation could continue. A more radical possibility is that psychic internets can take on a life of their own, so to speak, and exist independently of any living person, although with the power to draw people in (at a subconscious level) and use them on an ad hoc basis.

Of course, if the psychic internet theory (PIT) is valid, it doesn't necessarily mean that *all* genuinely anomalous UFO phenomena are produced in this way. Some UFOs could indeed be intelligently controlled craft from remote places, 'other dimensions', or even from our own future. Arguably, though, the PIT and the 'higher intelligence theory' (discussed below) are better able to explain the theatrical quality of many UFO sightings, and can more easily account for cases in which multifaceted and recurrent phenomena are associated with particular localities. The two theories aren't burdened by a need to demonstrate something physically unusual about UFO hot spots. They make no assumptions about special geological features or magnetic fields, and make no recourse to the 'subtle energies' that people of a New Age persuasion talk about. Similarly, they don't require the idea that UFO hot spots are 'portals' or gateways to other worlds.

However, given that collaboration and co-ordination are activities that we normally associate with consciousness, the notion that people's minds can interact at a subconscious level to orchestrate paranormal phenomena is somewhat hard to accept. But some sort of unconscious interaction between people seems to be indicated by telepathic experiences.

Arguably, though, if the PIT were true, there should be many more reports of miraculous healing. Take, for instance, Pope John Paul II, who died in April 2005 after years of poor health. Millions of Catholics no doubt prayed for him during his final years. With such widespread collective concern for his wellbeing, we might have expected large psychic internets to come into being, exerting a beneficial effect on his health. Similarly, in the case of families with very sick children, we might expect psychic internets to produce numerous dramatic cures. Sadly, though, there seems to be little or no evidence of that. Therefore, if psychic internets exist, there may be severe limits to what they can do: they may be much better at producing ephemeral phenomena (sightings of ghosts and UFOs, for example) than lasting physical effects of a positive kind.

Orchestrations of a higher intelligence

Anomalous UFO events may be dramatic performances staged by a higher, non-human intelligence. I'll refer to this as the higher intelligence theory (HIT). Although it represents my 'best bet' about what lies behind many UFO and paranormal events, and is in that sense 'my theory', it should be noted that other writers have advanced, or at least hinted at, similar notions.

Apart from suggesting a different source for the phenomena (a higher intelligence as opposed to collective subconscious activity in humans), the HIT is very similar to the PIT: for both theories, the supposed alien spaceships and extraterrestrial entities are essentially 'stage props' – choreographed hallucinations, transient materialisations or false memories.

From the perspective of the HIT, it isn't necessary to suppose that the intelligence behind the phenomena comes from another place, another time or another dimension – it may have always been with us. Similarly, since the UFOs and entities have no independent, continuing existence, there's no need to assume that they come from a distant planet, another dimension, a parallel reality or another time. Accordingly, this theory is more parsimonious than some of its competitors. Unlike the extraterrestrial hypothesis, the theory doesn't face the problem of accounting for the fact that UFOs appear in a bewildering array of shapes and sizes. It's no problem for the theory that UFOs sometimes change shape before people's eyes, or appear or disappear in an instant. Similarly, the theory isn't embarrassed by the fact that the occupants of UFOs sometimes have a very human-like appearance.

PHANTOM VEHICLES AND AIRCRAFT

The ghosts of supernatural fiction are typically restless, vengeful spirits, and – as I noted in the previous chapter – a spiritualist stance is adopted by many people who investigate supposedly real cases. However, the idea that apparitions are spirits (or representations of spirits) is challenged by cases involving ghostly appearances of inanimate objects, such as cars and aircraft. But it's hard to say what's behind these phenomena. Sightings of phantom vehicles and aircraft may perplex witnesses, but they're likely to be less traumatic than some of the phenomena that will be described later in this book.

I've arranged the following selection of cases in a roughly north-to-south order.

ENCOUNTERS IN NORTHERN SCOTLAND

Loch Ashie is a few miles south-south-west of Inverness, in an area that has allegedly been the setting for apparitions, including sightings of phantom soldiers or warriors.[1] Without giving a date, Major C.J. Shaw describes an occasion when he was driving with his wife in the locality and 'had the experience, in broad daylight, of slowing down at a corner where he had seen an approaching car which had signalled with his lights that he was pulling into a passing place, only to find the road empty!'[2]

Loch Ashie, near Inverness.

Paul Heinowski, from Inverness, has informed me about an experience that he had a few miles south-east of the loch, probably in the winter of 1973/74. His father was driving him to Flichity, so that he could visit a friend at the schoolhouse there. Heinowski writes:

> It was dark and we were [heading south] on the single-track road running from Dunlichity Churchyard, over the hill to join the Farr road [the B851]. We stopped opposite a house in order to ask directions and I saw headlights approaching, perhaps a quarter of a mile ahead of us. A high hedge surrounded the house and I could not see the road as I knocked on the door. However, I heard the car passing on the other side of the hedge. The house was empty; so I returned to the car.

Heinowski asked how the other car had managed to pass, but his father hadn't been aware of it. They eventually found the schoolhouse. Over a cup of tea, Heinowski's friend asked whether he'd heard about the phantom car. Looking at the road some years later, Heinowski noticed a side road leaving it more or less at the point where the headlights had first appeared. However, as noted, he believes that he heard the car going past on the other side of the hedge when he was attempting to ask for directions at a house. Furthermore, he was aware of the glow of its lights as it passed. Therefore, if these recollections are accurate, he may have had a paranormal hallucinatory experience.

In his book *Gazetteer of Scottish Ghosts*, Peter Underwood refers to sightings of a ghostly Austin car travelling at high speed 'along the hill road from Sligachan' on the Isle of Skye. He states that one of the first reports came from a Dr Allan MacDonald, who, in 1941, saw the car coming towards him at a terrific speed. MacDonald drew in to let the car pass, but saw no more of it.[3]

In 1999, a man working in a bar adjoining the Sligachan Hotel, which is located just north of the Cuillin mountains, told me of an occasion when he saw a car which then disappeared. I asked him to send me a written account of his experience, but I didn't receive one.

Dr Martin Moar informed me of an experience that he and a fellow climber had while driving on Skye in the early 1970s, although he couldn't recall the precise location. They pulled into a passing place to make way for an oncoming car. The passing place was just before a small hump in the road. The approaching car disappeared behind the hump, but didn't reappear, and there seemed to be nowhere it could have gone without being seen.

Moar forwarded me a letter – from February 1992 – that he'd received from a Mrs Helen Kirkland, who described a similar experience. It had occurred on the mainland in late 1945. I contacted her, and although she was by then relatively elderly, the event still seemed to be clear in her mind. She and her husband, a naval officer at the time of the incident, were being driven from a naval base at Aultbea in Wester Ross to Inverness, having departed around 6.30 a.m. The following is from her letter to Martin Moar:

> Our driver was a local man employed at the base. I sat in front, beside him, and my husband was in the back seat. We were travelling on a long stretch of road with moorland on either side. I could see a large vehicle with big, blazing headlights approaching, but it was then obscured by a small S-bend with outcrops of rock on both sides. Our driver pulled into a passing place and waited – and waited. I didn't think anything unusual was happening, because big naval transports were quite commonplace in that area. Eventually, we pulled out cautiously, and after negotiating the bend were confronted by the long,

straight road – which was absolutely empty! It was only when the driver asked me, in a shocked whisper, if I had seen it too that I began to think it very odd – even more so when my husband, who had been leaning forward, talking to us, said that he had seen nothing.

Mrs Kirkland's husband may have been too engrossed in his conversation with his wife and the driver to notice the oncoming vehicle. However, reports indicate that when apparitions appear, not everyone in a position to see them will necessarily do so.

Bill Paterson, from Edinburgh, informed me about an interesting experience that he'd had in the 1950s when he was nearly 5. He and members of his family were travelling to the Black Isle. They were on the old A9 road, and had just passed Slochd Summit in the central Highlands when Paterson's elder brother noticed an unusual locomotive, which Paterson then saw as well.[4] The engine was old-fashioned, like one from a Western film. It was coming up a gradient, from the Inverness direction,

Location of the sighting of a phantom locomotive in the Scottish Highlands.

belching smoke from the stack and exuding white smoke (steam?) from the sides. They asked their father to stop the car, so that they could see the locomotive, and he pulled up just past the bridge that crosses the railway line. Paterson notes that, 'We ran back to the bridge and looked over [but] there was nothing!' That was odd, because, in his estimation, they could probably see for a mile up and down the track. (I've visited the site and agree with that assessment.) They stopped at Inverness, but an enquiry at the railway station drew a blank: the stationmaster telephoned the signal box at Slochd, but was informed that nothing had been seen.

A VANISHING CAR IN SOUTHERN SCOTLAND

Kathleen Cronie is the founder of Mostly Ghostly Investigations, a group based in Dumfries, southern Scotland. After a letter of hers was published, appealing for ghost stories, she received an account from a female informant regarding an experience that had occurred on a Friday in September 2007, about 40 miles west-south-west of Dumfries.

It was a bright morning. The informant was driving to Newton Stewart on the A75. She explained that before the junction for Kirkcowan traffic (the one linking the A75 and the B735, I presume), there's a very bad bend and then a stretch of straight road that drivers use for overtaking. But there's an invisible dip, which can catch them out if they're not familiar with the road. After passing the bend, the informant had a good, clear view of the road ahead. Up to that point, she hadn't seen any other traffic going in either direction, which was unusual. But now, she saw, in the far distance, a large black car coming towards her. To improve her driving skills, she counted the seconds from when she saw it go into the dip, to judge how long she would have had to overtake a car at that point. However, the oncoming vehicle didn't reappear. Soon, the informant's own car entered the dip, but the other vehicle was nowhere to be seen. She felt a little perturbed, but thought that the other driver must have turned off the road. Returning home a couple of hours later, she made an effort to see where the black car had turned off. But there was no exit of any kind. She noted: 'It certainly gave me a shiver down my spine, and I can offer no explanation. What I can say, however, is that I don't normally notice cars at all, e.g. colour or make, etc., but I noticed this one, which is strange in itself as it seemed to be out of place somehow!!'

A DOUBLE SIGHTING IN WEST LANCASHIRE

Halsall Moss, in the administrative district of West Lancashire, is an area of flat, fertile farmland, reclaimed by drainage. It covers much of the western part of the civil parish of Halsall. Rob Gandy, a visiting professor at the Liverpool Business School, of Liverpool John Moores University, has collected a number of reports of people having road ghost experiences on, or near, the Moss.

In the late 1980s, a colleague of Gandy's described a ghostly experience that he'd had in 1965 while driving along Gregory Lane on Halsall Moss, between Southport and Ormskirk. The colleague subsequently met someone at a social event who reported having had a very similar experience on the same road.[5] I shall discuss these sightings in Chapter 4. In January 2015, the Southport, Ormskirk and West Lancashire issues of *The Champion*, a free newspaper, published a piece by Gandy under the heading: 'Doc's appeal to unravel mystery of ghostly hitchhiker.' It invited readers to provide him with first-hand or, at the very least, second-hand accounts of similar experiences

Halsall Moss, West Lancashire.

that might have occurred in the area. He received eight reports of interest.[6] One of them merits attention in this chapter.

The incident in question occurred in the summer of 2005, around 5.50 a.m. The informant, accompanied by her mother, was driving on the A570 towards Ormskirk. They were on a long, straight stretch outside Southport, travelling at approximately 30mph. A white van suddenly came alongside their car. The weather was warm and the informant had her window down, but there was no sound from the van. Its driver, a clean-shaven man, who looked about 40, smiled at the informant and her mother, and seemed to overtake them. But then, the van and its driver appeared to vanish into thin air. Within 2 minutes, it reappeared at the side of the car, with the same man driving it. Then, as before, it vanished. The informant noted that there were no turn-offs from the road and that the area was quite flat. Therefore, if it had been a real vehicle, it couldn't have left the road without being seen.

PHANTOM AIRCRAFT IN THE PEAK DISTRICT

A ghostly Lancaster bomber has reportedly been seen on several occasions skimming over the Ladybower Reservoir in the Derwent Valley in Derbyshire's Peak District. It is noteworthy that RAF bomber crews flew training sorties in the area prior to the 'Dambusters' raid on Germany in 1943. A typical sighting occurred one moonlit night in October 1982, and is described in David Clarke's book *Supernatural Peak District*. Driving home after visiting relatives in Glossop, a couple called Shaw pulled into a lay-by beside the reservoir for a breath of fresh air. Mr Shaw saw something flying across the water towards them. Then it swung round to his right and continued up the reservoir. He took it to be a hang-glider. It turned again and flew back towards the couple. A burst of moonlight revealed the outline of a Lancaster bomber of World War II vintage. After flying over the reservoir for about another 200 yards, it suddenly vanished, leaving the two witnesses stunned.[7]

David Clarke's book (p. 148) relates that one afternoon in April 1995, Tony Ingle was walking with his golden retriever along Aston Lane in Hope, Derbyshire, when he saw what appeared to be a wartime aircraft flying 40–60ft above him. Ingle reportedly saw the propellers turning, but there was no sound. The plane was getting lower, and he saw it banking. Then, it appeared to go down over a hedge. Ingle ran up the lane, expecting

Ladybower Reservoir, Derbyshire.

to see the plane in a field, but there were just sheep and lambs there, and everything was eerily silent. He returned to Aston Lane many times, but his dog always refused to go anywhere near the field concerned. Ingle's sighting is also mentioned by Alan Baker, in his book *Ghosts and Spirits*, but he gives a different date for it: 5 May 1994.[8]

A STRANGE EXPERIENCE IN STAFFORDSHIRE

At lunchtime on 29 July 2005, Cherill Royce-Dexter (or Cherill Penton, as she was then) had an apparitional experience at the junction of Borough Lane and Horsey Lane in Rugeley, Staffordshire. She wrote an account of it that same day and posted it on the Internet forum of the Paranormal Awakening Scientific Study Association, a group that she had co-founded. She was in her car, driving back from Longdon Green, as she usually did at that time on a Friday. Normally, by the time she reached the junction, there would be an elderly man on his bicycle and one or two horse riders on the roads. But on this occasion, the roads were empty. It was a fairly pleasant day and she had her driver's side window three-quarters of the way down. She approached the junction with a view to turning left, and heard the sound of a horse's hooves clopping on the road to her right. The sound seemed louder than usual. After what seemed a long wait, a horse and carriage with a single driver appeared right in front of her, out of nowhere. The driver, a man, was wearing a brown cloak and a hat. Behind the driver's seat was a double seat for passengers. The horse was fairly sturdy, of a chestnut colour, and had a plaited mane. The man looked at Royce-Dexter, tipped his hat, and smiled. Then, the vision suddenly vanished.

A DRIVERLESS TRUCK ON THE M6 MOTORWAY

In his book *Haunted Land*, Paul Devereux describes a phantom vehicle encounter that he had early one morning in 1980. He was driving on the M6 motorway near Birmingham, on his way to London. He pulled into the central lane to let a mini-pickup truck join the main carriageway from a slip road without having to slow down. Passing it, he glanced idly at the driver's cab, which appeared empty. He peered more intently, but saw no sign of the driver. He sped on until he was level with a white van and then glanced in his rear-view mirror. The motorway behind him was empty. Although his view wasn't impeded, he dropped back well behind the white van and looked around. However, there was no other vehicle to be seen, and there were no exit points by which the mysterious truck could have left the carriageway.[9]

A VANISHING CAR IN NORTHAMPTONSHIRE

Some years ago, I was in touch with a woman from Northamptonshire called Roberta Abbott. She informed me, among other things, about two experiences that she'd had featuring phantom cars. The first one may have been in the mid-1960s. She was driving out of Northampton on the A428, through the suburb of Duston. In her rear-view mirror, she saw a silver car pull out to overtake her, but when she then looked in her side mirror, it wasn't there. She looked in the rear-view mirror again, but no car was in sight. When she looked back over each shoulder, no car was to be seen.

Abbott's second phantom car experience wasn't in Northamptonshire. But, for convenience, I'll mention it here. It happened a year or two after her first experience. She couldn't recall the precise location, but she thought that it was in Hampshire or Dorset. The incident was very similar to the first experience, but the overtaking car was red, not grey. She informed me that there were no turnings on either side of the road that the car could have taken.

A GHOSTLY REPLAY?

On the evening of 11 December 2002, members of the public informed the Surrey police that they'd seen a car lose control and swerve off the southbound carriageway of the busy A3 at Burpham, near Guildford. Police attended the scene and at first saw nothing unusual. However, a further search resulted in a grim discovery: 20 yards from the road, lying nose-down in a ditch and shrouded by undergrowth, was a crashed car. The skeletal and decomposed remains of the driver were also found. According to a *Mail Online* article, they were *inside* the car, but this is contradicted by other sources. A *Telegraph* article of 12 August 2003 reports that the driver, 'Christopher Chandler, [...] crawled from his Vauxhall Astra, but could not climb the bank of the A3 [...] to seek help'. It was believed that the accident had occurred in July 2002, when the 20- or 21-year-old driver (the sources differ regarding his precise age) was reported missing. He was apparently on the run from the police.

Unfortunately, only limited information seems to be available about what members of the public initially reported to the police. Sergeant Russ Greenhouse of the Surrey police is quoted in the *Mail Online* article as stating, 'The car was discovered as a result of a report from members of the public who thought they saw a car's headlights veering off the road.' Of course, this raises the intriguing possibility that the witnesses experienced an apparitional 'replay' of something that had happened months previously.[10]

GENERAL COMMENTS

Some people appear to be more psychic than others, and it may be that they unwittingly act as catalysts for ghostly manifestations. If so, being in the presence of such a person might increase one's likelihood of having a paranormal experience. Roberta Abbott told me about various unusual experiences in her life in addition to her encounters with phantom cars. For example, she explained that there had been ghostly phenomena in her home. A young woman, who'd been a frequent visitor to the house, confirmed to me that she had also experienced phenomena there.

It can be seen that there's quite a bit of variation in these reported phantom vehicle experiences. In two of the accounts mentioned above, the apparitional driver of the phantom vehicle acted as if he were aware of the witnesses: the man in the white van seen in the West Lancashire case smiled at the witnesses, and the man seen by Cherill Royce-Dexter in Rugeley tipped his hat and smiled at her. However, the mini-pickup truck seen by Paul Devereux on the M6 motorway appeared to be driverless. Arguably, though, all of these experiences were alike, in that the manifestations were attention-grabbing and theatrical.

COLLIDING APPARITIONS

Imagine that you're driving along and that a pedestrian walks out in front of your car. You quickly apply the brakes, but there's insufficient time to avoid a collision. Feeling anxious and shocked, you get out, fully expecting to find a badly mangled body – but there's no one there, and your car is undamaged. You call the police. They conduct a search, but find no sign of an injured person.

Incidents of this type – with variations, of course – have been reported widely in Britain over the years, and they probably occur worldwide. Certain stretches of road seem to be hot spots for such activity. This chapter presents a selection of cases. I shall refer to the phantom figures as *colliding apparitions*, and I'll also include examples of 'near misses' – where drivers took evasive action and avoided hitting the ghostly figures. It goes without saying that if drivers brake or swerve suddenly to avoid phantom figures, they could put themselves and other road users at risk of having serious accidents.

THE LOCH ASHIE AREA NEAR INVERNESS

In the previous chapter, I noted that the Loch Ashie area, near Inverness, has reportedly hosted ghostly phenomena, including sightings of apparitional soldiers or warriors. Without giving a date, Neil Fraser-Tytler refers to an occasion when a man in that area, cycling to Inverness, saw three horsemen on the road ahead. Rounding a sharp bend, 'he ran into and through them. He fell off his bicycle with astonishment, and on getting up he beheld the phantom armies.'[1] Major C.J. Shaw mentions a story about a cyclist 'meeting *four* horsemen who disappeared as they rode through him' (my emphasis).[2] Of course, this may be a different version of the story mentioned by Fraser–Tytler.

After mentioning the Loch Ashie case during a lecture to the Society for Psychical Research in 2003, I was told about someone who'd reportedly had a ghostly experience in the area. I wrote to the percipient's mother, who lived not far from the loch, asking her to pass on to her son (the alleged witness) a letter and an enclosed stamped addressed envelope. My hope was that he would supply first-hand testimony. However, I received no reply, and I don't know whether he ever received my letter. During a telephone conversation in June 2004, his mother told me that the incident had occurred around 10.30 p.m. on 1 May when her son was driving home, but she couldn't recall the year. She said that he saw a bubble of mist with a woman in it, whose eyes and teeth were lit up, and that he drove through it without stopping.

THE A75 ROAD IN SOUTHERN SCOTLAND

From its junction with the M74 motorway, the A75 road snakes west to Stranraer. Over the years, the stretch between Gretna and Dumfries (approximately 23 miles) has generated a number of reports of colliding apparitions, and also accounts of other types of ghostly manifestation. However, so far as I know, the sightings between Gretna and Annan have all been on, or close to, the route of the *old* A75 rather than on the present-day A75. This part of the old A75 is now designated as the B721. Going west from Gretna, it runs through Rigg, Eastriggs, Dornock and Annan before joining the A75. The eastern part of the modern-day A75 is to the north, and bypasses these population centres.

Haunted sites in fictional films typically appear atmospheric and spooky. But with supposedly real paranormal events, the settings are often unassuming. That's true of the stretch of road considered here. In places, the peaks of the northern Lake District can be seen to the south, but the scenery is generally unremarkable.

The B721 road at Eastriggs.

The A75 road between Annan and Dumfries.

The A75 phenomena have been mentioned in books, in newspaper articles, and on the Internet. But some of these sources are very inaccurate. For example, an Internet post by a Mandy Collins begins by stating, 'The Kinmount Straight on the A75 between Annan and Gretna in Dumfries and Galloway is a road where the unexpected happens.'[3] In fact, the Kinmount Straight *isn't* between Annan and Gretna – it is west-north-west of Annan. ('The Kinmount Straight' seems to be a local, informal designation for a relatively straight part of the A75 that begins about a mile west of Annan and ends at, or near, the hamlet of Carrutherstown, to the west-north-west. It's approximately 5 miles long.)

Incidents in the 1950s

The 29 October 2010 edition of the *Annandale Observer* contained an article by Rod Edgar, its chief reporter, concerning the A75 apparitions. He refers to a Jim Carlyle, who was 75 at the time of Edgar's writing. Carlyle had had an apparitional experience one night in 1955 while driving a taxi from Eastriggs to Annan, accompanied by his future wife. Edgar quotes him as saying: 'There was a woman, dressed in white, a long cape, and she just floated right across the road in front of me. I braked, but I went right through her – it was a ghost.' Edgar doesn't say whether Carlyle's future wife also saw the figure.

Annan, southern Scotland.

The late Andrew Green described an experience reported by a lorry driver called Hugh Watson Reid. The incident had allegedly occurred at 10.45 p.m. one misty night in October 1957. The location appears to have been Gretna, although Green's article refers to it, mistakenly, as Gretna Green. As Reid reached a bend in the road, at the junction with the A75, he saw a middle-aged couple walk arm-in-arm in front of his lorry. The man was wearing a high tile hat, a short double-breasted jacket and tight trousers. His companion was wearing a crinoline ankle-length gown and a large hat of the sun-bonnet type. Reid brought his lorry and trailer to a halt, switched on the hazard warning lights, and jumped out, intending to remonstrate with the careless couple. But they'd vanished. There hadn't been time for them to jump clear of the vehicle, and there was no sign of them beneath it. Furthermore, an impenetrable hedge bordered the road at that spot.[4]

Incidents in the 1960s

In his newspaper article of 29 October 2010, Rod Edgar refers to a Margaret Ching, who'd allegedly had a sighting in 1960. However, Kathleen Cronie, the founder of the Dumfries-based group Mostly Ghostly Investigations, informs me that another newspaper article has placed that sighting in the 1990s. It's therefore possible that Edgar got the date wrong in his October 2010 piece. At any rate, he states that Margaret Ching 'was approaching Dornock, travelling to Gretna with her fiancé, when she saw an old woman in Victorian clothes standing in the middle of the road.' The couple thought that they'd driven straight through her, and they described feeling a terrible chill.

The late Peter Underwood's book *Gazetteer of Scottish Ghosts* recounts a very dramatic story about two brothers, Derek and Norman Ferguson, although I don't know whether those are their real names – or, indeed, whether they really existed. The incident supposedly occurred one night in April 1962 as they were driving from Dumfries towards Annan. A large hen flew towards their car, only to disappear when it would have been expected to strike the windscreen. Shortly after, an old woman rushed towards the car, waving her arms. But she also vanished just when she would have been expected to collide with it. A succession of other figures appeared from nowhere (great cats, wild-looking dogs, goats, etc.). Derek, who was 22 at the time, swerved and braked repeatedly, trying to miss the spectres. He noticed that none of them actually hit the car, and he initially thought that it must all have been his imagination. But when he glanced at his 14-year-old brother, he realised that Norman was seeing them as well. They were aware of a drop in temperature in the car, and Derek felt as if a force were trying to take control of the steering wheel. The brothers felt as if they were suffocating, but when Derek opened a window, it was bitterly cold outside. Screaming, high-pitched laugher and cackling noises were reportedly heard. Derek eventually stopped the car, but then it seemed to be bounced up and down and rocked from side to side, which made them dizzy. Derek felt very sick and leapt out, whereupon everything was quiet. But when he got back in and slammed the door, the shaking and high-pitched laughter resumed. A strong wind seemed to blow up, and there was a sensation of fists striking the vehicle. Driving on, they experienced more apparitions and frightening noises. Eventually, they observed a small, red gleam ahead. As they drew closer, it appeared to be the tail light of a large furniture van. Derek then realised that he was approaching it far too quickly, but found himself unable to take any evasive action — his foot wouldn't move from the accelerator pedal. But as they were seemingly about to crash into the van, it disappeared. As they drove on, Derek noticed that the car had slowed to a crawl, and that the noises and high wind had died away. Subsequently, Derek spoke to a friend, who'd been stationed near Annan during military service in World War II. Allegedly, he'd often heard stories of witchcraft being practised in the area. Another friend had reportedly read of a phantom furniture van being seen thereabouts.[5]

Underwood's book doesn't specify his source for this dramatic tale. I'm doubtful about its historical accuracy. Indeed, in a letter to me in 2011, Underwood admitted that he was 'never completely happy with the story'. It's certainly not typical. For one thing, road ghost experiences are generally much briefer. The Fergusons' ordeal supposedly went on for nearly half an hour. But there's no mention of their encountering any other traffic during that period, apart from the apparitional furniture van. Admittedly, the incident is said to have occurred late at night; and there were, of course, fewer vehicles on Britain's roads in 1962. But I imagine that the A75 would have been fairly busy even then.

Incidents in the 1990s

Kathleen Cronie informed me about an experience reported by a taxi driver. Jim (pseudonym) and his wife were driving along the Dumfries bypass, heading out towards Collin, which is to the east of Dumfries. About a quarter of a mile away, he saw what looked like a woman in green by the roadside.

The road ahead was clear. As he and his wife approached, the figure walked into the road. Jim hit the brakes and his wife went through the same motions in the passenger seat, bracing herself for impact. The figure disappeared. Jim and his wife drove around the next roundabout and back, to see if they could find any trace of the woman, but there was no sign of her. The sighting reportedly occurred not long after the Dumfries bypass had opened, which I understand (from Kathleen Cronie) was in 1990 or 1991.

In March 1995, a couple called Garson and Monica Miller were driving towards Annan on the Kinmount Straight when the figure of a man jumped out in front of them. They were apparently convinced that their vehicle had made contact with the figure, and they immediately notified the police. In his article in the 29 October 2010 edition of the *Annandale Observer*, Rod Edgar writes: 'Looking back on the experience this week, Monica [...] said: "What I saw appeared in front of the car dressed in a cloak, like a monk's habit. And he was holding what looked like a sock [*sic*] with something in it."' (I presume that 'sock' is a misprint of 'sack'.)

An article in the 1 August 1997 edition of the *Annandale Observer* described an incident that had occurred about two weeks previously. Donna Maxwell, 27, was driving home to Annan from Eastriggs on the old A75 when a man seemed to jump out in front of her car. She slammed on her brakes and closed her eyes for a second, but heard nothing. When she opened her eyes, she saw that the man had vanished. She was accompanied by her two children, who reportedly also witnessed the incident. The newspaper article quotes a police spokesman as stating that they'd been unable to trace the man, and that it was still a complete mystery. According to an Internet article, which no longer seems to be available, Maxwell reported that: 'Since [the incident] I have heard other people talking about seeing the same man standing in the road just looking at the cars.' The article also quoted her as stating: 'I was convinced I hit [the man] but I couldn't see anyone so I drove to Annan police station.' However, this conflicts with the above-mentioned newspaper account, which says that she drove home before she and her husband contacted the police.

In respect of the Maxwell sighting, Graeme Wellburn, Public Information Officer with the Dumfries and Galloway Constabulary, informed me that, 'Having lived [in] and policed the Annan area for some 32 years myself I cannot recall any other such incidents in that area' (e-mail, February 2011). As noted above, though, Garson and Monica Miller reportedly contacted the police after their sighting in March 1995. In any case, witnesses don't always report such incidents to the police.

Incident in 2010

Derek McCall, then a member of the aforementioned group Mostly Ghostly Investigations (MGI), encountered a colliding apparition on 12 December 2010, between 8.20 and 8.25 p.m., while driving on the western fringe of Dumfries. He was travelling at 60mph and listening to the radio. The figure of an elderly woman suddenly appeared at the side of the road. She wandered into the road in front of him. McCall hit the brakes. If the figure had been a flesh-and-blood person, there wouldn't have been time to avoid a collision. But the figure simply vanished. McCall checked his rear-view mirror, but there was nothing to be seen.[6]

Coincidentally, the previous night, McCall and his fellow investigators had been in the area of the A75/B721 sightings, and had been discussing them. Was this ghostly encounter somehow staged for his benefit? MGI's Kathleen Cronie informs me that she regards McCall as a credible witness, and that she remembers how ashen he looked when he came to pick her up that night. She thinks that he was still in shock. She explained to me that McCall told the team that the woman was already in the process of walking when he first saw her – it wasn't a case of her standing for a couple of seconds and then walking out into the road.

A bear-like figure

Kathleen Cronie relayed another report to me that she'd received from a taxi driver, but she can't recall his mentioning a date. The incident didn't involve a colliding apparition, but it's of interest nonetheless. The man was going to work, and heading for Annan. It was a foggy morning, so he was keeping his speed down. He entered the Kinmount Straight, which many motorists use for overtaking. On reaching a point where there are trees on both sides of the road, he saw a bear-like creature crossing from left to right. But when he looked back, the form had become that of a woman. He said that a lot of stories about the 'bear' and a phantom woman had done the rounds locally.

Comments

In January 2011, I called in at the offices of the *Annandale Observer* and spoke to Rod Edgar, the chief reporter. He indicated that he had contact details for some of the witnesses – at least two, as I recall – and I was hoping that he'd pass that information on to me, if they gave their consent. He said that he would try to contact them on my behalf. But, despite reminders, he didn't get back to me. I also submitted a short article to the paper about the apparitions, inviting readers to contact me if they had anything interesting to report. But I had no formal response from the paper, and I presume that they didn't publish my piece.

Obviously, I can't guarantee that the above-mentioned events occurred as described. And it's hard to know whether the number of genuine incidents on, or near, the A75 and B721 has been any higher than elsewhere, because we don't have reliable comparative statistics about the distribution of such events. On the other hand, the testimony of a Bob Sturgeon suggests that apparitional phenomena, not confined to incidents of the 'colliding' type, may have been, and possibly still are, quite frequent in the area. A BBC website article of 25 October 2013 by Willie Johnston quotes Sturgeon, who used to run a roadside snack van at Carrutherstown, close to the Kinmount Straight. At that time, according to Sturgeon, rarely a week went past without somebody telling him about an experience, and usually it had happened on the Kinmount Straight. An experience commonly reported by traumatised lorry drivers who'd parked overnight in nearby lay-bys was of seeing groups of dejected, bedraggled people pulling handcarts or carrying bundles, like medieval camp followers. One witness was so shocked that he gave up lorry driving altogether, and Sturgeon never saw him again. He'd apparently woken up in the early hours of the morning to see a parade of people, and the vision had lasted a long time.[7]

HALSALL MOSS, WEST LANCASHIRE

Judging from reports gathered by Rob Gandy, West Lancashire has been the setting for multiple road ghost experiences.[8] One of them, involving a phantom white van and driver, was mentioned in the previous chapter. Gandy's collection also includes a report of a colliding apparition encountered on Halsall Moss. The witness, referred to as Alan, was a taxi driver, and the incident occurred between 3 and 3.30 a.m. on a Sunday in June or July in the late 1990s. Alan, who was feeling tired at the time, was driving west on Gregory Lane from Halsall Village towards Birkdale when the figure of 'an oldish guy wearing a cap' suddenly appeared in front of his vehicle.

Alan slammed on the brakes, but the figure had been so close that Alan was sure that he'd run over the man. However, when he got out and checked, there was no sign of the pedestrian. Of course, given that Alan was feeling tired, it's possible that he experienced a hallucination arising from sleep deprivation. If so, there may have been nothing paranormal about the incident.

THE STOCKSBRIDGE BYPASS, SOUTH YORKSHIRE

Ghostly events allegedly occurred during the construction of the Stocksbridge bypass (the A616), which began in the autumn of 1987. But sources differ about some of the precise details, and the authenticity of some of the stories has been questioned.[9] Following the official opening of the bypass in May 1988, people continued to report ghostly experiences in the locality. For example, in his book about paranormal phenomena in the Peak District, David Clarke mentions an incident involving a couple who were travelling on the bypass on New Year's Eve, 1997. From a distance, 28-year-old Paul Ford, who was doing the driving, saw what appeared to be someone trying to cross the road. When he got nearer, it looked like a man in a long cloak. Then he noticed that the figure had no face and was hovering *above* the road! He braked hard and swerved, to avoid hitting it. The car would have crashed if his wife hadn't grabbed the steering wheel.[10]

The bypass acquired some notoriety as a result of fatal accidents, although I don't know whether any of them were caused by apparitions. But the status of the bypass as one of Britain's most dangerous roads has been questioned.[11]

THE A15 NEAR RUSKINGTON, LINCOLNSHIRE

A section of the A15 in Lincolnshire, eastern England, has been the setting for road ghost sightings.[12] This apparent hot spot is about 12 miles south-south-east of Lincoln and some 4 miles north-north-west of Sleaford, close to a junction with a minor road that goes east from the A15 towards the village of Ruskington. In 1998, the subject of ghosts was featured in an episode of *This Morning*, an ITV programme. A man named Kevin Whelan rang in and described an experience that he'd had a fortnight previously on the A15. Numerous other people then called to report ghostly encounters there, but only a minority of them were willing to be identified. Interviews were conducted locally, and the case featured in further editions of the programme. In addition to Whelan's sighting, I'll describe a few other incidents from the locality that conform to the colliding apparition type.

Kevin Whelan's experience

Whelan's sighting occurred around 2 a.m. on a Sunday while he was driving from Lincoln to Sleaford on the A15. After negotiating a sharp bend, and before reaching the junction with the minor road going left to Ruskington, he saw something on the horizon, 'like a white shadow'. When he reached that point, a face suddenly emerged from around the driver's side pillar of his vehicle and came on to the windscreen. It had dark hair, like that of a Greek person. The skin appeared 'olivey-green', and the face was pitted. The figure's left hand was held up. Whelan could see its teeth, and the face bore an expression of considerable distress. 'From the neck down [it] was like a sort of – on a photograph when you photograph someone with a flash on [... and] you get that white fluorescent sort of look.' Eventually, the figure faded away down the side of the vehicle. Arriving home, Whelan woke his wife, to tell her about his experience. Interviewed by a reporter from *This Morning*, she said that she'd never seen her husband in such a distraught state before.

A black silhouette

An informant called Sarah Martin told *This Morning* about an experience that she'd had the previous year (1997), although when she was interviewed the next day, she gave the year as 1996. She and her boyfriend had been at a cinema in Lincoln, and were heading home to Cranwell. A black silhouette, which she thought was probably that of a man, ran out in front of their car from a ditch. They went through it. But her boyfriend, who was doing the driving, didn't see it. She said that this happened at exactly the same spot as where Kevin Whelan had had his experience.[13]

Collision with an inanimate form

In the case of at least one witness, Jenny Sellars, the colliding apparition wasn't of an obviously animate figure. Her experience occurred while she was driving from Sleaford to Lincoln in about 1988 or 1989. She wasn't going particularly fast, because the stretch of road was quite dark. What she thought was a sheet, or piece of plastic, came down in front of her windscreen, inducing her to brake hard, although she didn't feel any impact. As she stopped the car, 'it went round the side of the window', although when she opened the door to look, she saw nothing.

A traumatised taxi driver

I obtained the following story from Garry Ross, who founded a group called the Lincs Paranormal Research Team (LincsPRT) in 2003.[14] In the spring of that year, they heard about a woman, in her early 40s, who'd reportedly given up her job as a taxi driver the day after seeing an apparition on the A15. The information came from a woman at a Lincoln taxi firm, who was at the control desk most of the time. The team never got to interview the driver herself, so the details were obtained only second-hand, although the police confirmed that the incident had happened.

The sighting had occurred two weeks previously, around 1 a.m. The woman was driving back to Lincoln. After she passed the Ruskington turn-off, a figure ran in front her car. (This spot, a little to the north of the turn-off, is where other incidents have occurred. For example, Kevin Whelan's experience – described above – apparently began thereabouts, although he was driving the other way, towards Sleaford.) The figure looked straight at the woman, with an open mouth, as if screaming, and then vanished under the vehicle, although the driver felt no impact. She stopped and looked around, but saw nothing unusual. Terrified, she called the police (via a mobile phone or a radio in her vehicle, I presume), who checked the location, but also saw nothing of note. The woman was so traumatised that the police drove her home. Someone else drove her car home for her. The witness claimed that she hadn't been speeding when she saw the ghostly figure. The police confirmed to LincsPRT that they'd received several similar reports over the years.

Comments

Regarding the other hot spots discussed in this chapter, the apparitions haven't all been of the 'colliding' type. The same is true of this part of Lincolnshire. For example, an informant named Catherine Stephenson told *This Morning* about an incident that had occurred when she was 15, when she used to walk to Ruskington, to go to school. She felt a shiver go up her back, and turned round to see a figure that was 'like a head and shoulders', although she didn't see any arms. But from the waist down, it was like a sheet. The figure had emerged from a ditch.

SLITTING MILL ROAD, CANNOCK CHASE

Cannock Chase is a 26-square-mile area of woodland and heath lying to the south-east of Stafford. It's part of what was once a large hunting ground created by William the Conqueror and known as the King's Forest of Cannock. The development of settlements in the Middle Ages led to the clearing of woodland, which gathered pace in the sixteenth century, when trees were destroyed to produce charcoal. Fortunately, there's still a scattering of oaks, which are most abundant in Brocton Coppice, in the north-western part of the Chase. But much of the woodland is now coniferous rather than broadleaf.

In a short book about strange events reportedly experienced on Cannock Chase, Lee Brickley refers to an apparition seen by a female motorist around

Brocton Coppice, Cannock Chase.

midnight in February 2010.[15] Caroline Parks was driving on Slitting Mill Road, between the towns of Hednesford and Rugeley, when a figure materialised in the middle of the road, some 10ft in front of her. She almost crashed her car while swerving to avoid it. When her car came to a stop, she looked back through the rear window. The figure, which was almost translucent and had bright yellow eyes, looked like a man in a long black coat, wearing some sort of brimmed hat. She couldn't see where his legs met the road – it looked as if he were floating above it. Soon after, the figure disappeared into the surrounding woodland.

Parks related the incident to her parents when she got home. They said that her uncle had seen a similar figure while cycling home on that stretch of road one evening some 20 years previously. The figure was standing in the trees with its back to the road. When the uncle called out to enquire whether the person was all right, the figure apparently floated up and disappeared. Lee Brickley states that there have been other sightings of such a figure in the vicinity, and that he learned of five from 2012 alone. Three of these resembled Caroline Parks' sighting, in that the figure was dressed in black and was seen to be hovering above the ground. Another resembled the uncle's sighting, with a dark figure standing just inside the tree line and disappearing when an attempt at communication was made.

OLDNALL ROAD, WEST MIDLANDS

For many years, David and Carolyn Taylor ran Parasearch, a Midlands-based group that investigated the paranormal. It ceased operating in December 2016. In an interesting article, the Taylors discuss apparitional phenomena that have been experienced on Oldnall Road, which stretches for 2 miles between the towns of Halesowen and Stourbridge.[16]

The case came to their attention via a fellow member of Parasearch. A work colleague of his had had a frightening experience while driving on Oldnall Road after dark. His headlights illuminated a small child, possibly a girl, standing in the middle of the road. He swerved, and his vehicle mounted the grass verge before coming to a stop. When the shocked and panic-stricken driver looked back, there was no one on the road, and a frantic search revealed nothing. As noted at the beginning of this chapter, such incidents raise the possibility that apparitions have been responsible for serious accidents. The Taylors' article states that Oldnall Road is a

Oldnall Road. (K. Goodman)

notorious accident blackspot, despite being relatively straight and having no adverse camber. However, David Taylor informed me (email, November 2016) that he eventually noticed that the road *does* have an adverse camber. This discovery was presumably made after the article had been posted on the Internet.

Parasearch sent a press release to a local newspaper, inviting people to get in touch if they'd had similar experiences. The first to respond, Nick Harrison,[17] related that in early 2008 he and his wife were driving on the road and had to swerve to avoid the figure of a small boy, who looked about 10 years old and had a distinctly Victorian appearance. However, in some of the reports that Parasearch received, the apparitions weren't described as standing in the road or otherwise acting in a way likely to cause an accident. For example, Susan Goodwin[18] related that her aunt and uncle were driving along the road in 2004 and saw a man leading a large horse, although when they looked back, there was no sign of the man or horse.

The Taylors mention a dramatic sighting that wasn't from Oldnall Road itself, but from nearby Foxcote Lane. On an October evening in 2005, as he was driving home, Tony Griffiths braked sharply when the figure of a Victorian man with blurred facial features stepped out from a hedgerow into the path of his car. The figure walked through the front of the car and vanished through the opposite hedge. The event was also witnessed by the driver of a car behind Griffiths' vehicle.

Comments

Carolyn and David Taylor refer to a local archaeologist who has uncovered thousands of pieces of Mesolithic flint in the fields adjacent to Oldnall Road. However, that may have no bearing on the apparitional phenomena. After all, the English Midlands have been inhabited for centuries, and it's quite possible that artefacts could be found all over the region if people looked hard enough for them.

The Taylors' article states that the ancient parish boundary runs along Oldnall Road, and they refer to a study carried out by the folklorist Jeremy Harte regarding allegedly haunted road locations in Dorset.[19] He reports that a disproportionate number of the events (39 per cent) occurred within a tenth of a mile of parish boundaries. He based his analysis on seventy or so 'hauntings', although he seems to use that term loosely, in a way that includes what may have been one-off events rather than recurrent manifestations. Furthermore, only 18 cases were based on accounts of actual experiences (I presume that he's referring to first-hand accounts). With the other 'hauntings', the ghost story was either 'mere tradition' or 'a report that someone actually saw the ghost'.[20] By the latter, Harte presumably means a story that wasn't first-hand, but which involved at least one identified witness. Regarding the 18 'hauntings' of the first type, he reports that 54 per cent were within a tenth of a mile of a parish boundary. Of course, if cases were distributed randomly, some would occur near parish boundaries just by chance. Harte concedes that that would happen – in about 20 per cent of cases, in his estimation. He states that Dorset's parishes can be seen as irregular polygons, averaging 2,300 acres each, and that '[if] they were square, 20 percent of their area would be within 0.1 mile of the perimeter' (p. 7, n. 45). However, it's conceivable that, on average, *more than 20 per cent* of the terrain within the parishes is within 0.1 mile of the perimeter. Imagine, for example, a parish with an area of 4 square miles. If it were in the shape of a perfect square, each side would be 2 miles long, and the overall perimeter would be 8 miles. But if it were shaped as a right-angled triangle with a base of 1 mile and a height of 8 miles, its perimeter would be considerably longer, and more of the land within it would be close to the perimeter. If ghostly events occurred at random within it, we would expect more of them to be close to the perimeter than in the case of a square-shaped parish with the same area. Therefore, it's hard to know whether Harte has correctly estimated the percentage of cases in Dorset that, on a chance basis alone, might have been expected to occur near parish boundaries. Furthermore, he doesn't appear to have conducted a formal statistical analysis, and his findings would need to be replicated in other areas before we could confidently generalise from them.

I should explain that Harte's study wasn't confined to just one type of road ghost manifestation (e.g. colliding apparitions – indeed, I don't know whether any of his cases were of that type). It was more general, including, for example, alleged sightings of black dogs and phantom coaches.

Harte doesn't offer a clear explanation of *why* being on or near a parish boundary might increase one's likelihood of having a ghostly experience, but he suggests that it may have something to do with 'liminality' (being in a literal or metaphorical transition zone). But to my mind, that's tantamount to treating a descriptive aspect ('It happened near a boundary') as a cause ('It happened *because* the witness was near a boundary'). If a disproportionate number of road ghost experiences really do occur on, or near, parish boundaries, there could be more tangible reasons. For example, it could be that the busier roads in parishes tend to be on, or near, their boundaries. If so, a greater number of road ghost experiences would be expected to occur there.

THE RED BRIDGE, NEAR LLANIDLOES, MID WALES

Janet and Colin Bord give details of an interesting case from Mid Wales, their sources are reports from a Mid Wales newspaper, *The County Times and Express*.[21] Bill Hopkins, a primary school headmaster, encountered an apparition while driving home one night in May 1973. He was approaching an old railway bridge, known as the Red Bridge, 2 miles from Llanidloes, Powys, when a girl stepped out of a hedge into the path of his vehicle, although there was no sense of impact. He could see her sorrowful face looking straight at him, and it seemed to pass through his car. He inferred that she must have turned round, because he could still see her face in the mirror. The incident was publicised, and other people claimed to have seen the apparition in previous years. Then, in July of that year, just weeks after Hopkins' experience, Abderrahman Sennah, a chef, had a similar experience there.

BLUE BELL HILL, KENT

Blue Bell Hill is located on the North Downs, between Rochester and Maidstone. It's a chalk hill. The area bears the scars of overpopulation and over-development, with two motorways, the M2 and the M20, nearby, and another busy road, the A229, running over the hill between them, following the route of a former Roman road. The North Downs Tunnel carries a part of the Channel Tunnel Rail Link under the hill, and a village – itself called Blue Bell Hill – is situated on it. There are TV masts on the hill, and it's been speculated that their emissions may have affected drivers' brains, engendering anomalous experiences. There are also items of archaeological interest on the hill, including Kit's Coty House, which is thought to be the remains of a Neolithic (late Stone Age) burial tomb.

Over the years, the Blue Bell Hill (BBH) area has been the setting for various types of apparitional experience, including collision cases. The foremost authority on the BBH incidents is probably Sean Tudor, who has written articles on the subject,[22] and has interesting information about BBH on his website (referenced in n.12). He has recently (March 2017) published a detailed book on the BBH phantoms and similar cases from elsewhere, entitled *The Ghosts of Blue Bell Hill & other Road Ghosts*.

In this chapter, I'll describe four cases from BBH: two involving typical colliding apparitions; one in which the colliding figure was possibly an actual person; and one case of a somewhat different character. I'm including the latter to convey some idea of how varied the reports from BBH have been. Details of many other reported incidents involving BBH can be found in Tudor's book. The page numbers cited refer to it.

The site of Ian Sharpe's ghostly encounter on the A229 at Blue Bell Hill. (S. Tudor)

The experiences of Ian Sharpe and Christopher Dawkins

A little before midnight on 8 November 1992, 54-year-old Ian Sharpe was driving down Blue Bell Hill on the southbound carriageway of the A229 when he saw a young woman some distance ahead in the road. She ran in front of his car from the right, her face turned towards him. His vehicle seemed to hit her on her left side, and she disappeared beneath the car. But when Sharpe got out and checked, there was nothing to be seen (pp. 21–22).

On 22 November 1992, two weeks after Sharpe's encounter, 19-year-old Christopher Dawkins experienced something very similar while driving home to Maidstone. The incident occurred at 10.55 p.m. as he was passing the Robin Hood Lane junction in Blue Bell Hill village. He saw a woman run in front of his car. She stopped and looked at him with an expressionless face. Then, his Toyota car seemed to hit her. But, as in the Sharpe case, there was no evidence of a body or of damage to the vehicle (pp. 36–40).

Maurice Goodenough's experience

A bricklayer called Maurice Goodenough had an unusual experience while driving on Blue Bell Hill late one night in July 1974 (pp. 24–30). He was 35 years old at the time. Sources differ regarding some of the precise details, so I can't guarantee that the following summary is completely accurate, although it should give a fair impression of what reportedly happened.

On the night in question, Goodenough rushed into the police station in Rochester, Kent, to report an accident. He related that a girl, whom he estimated to be about 10 years old, had appeared in his headlights. Despite braking hard, he'd been unable to avoid running into her. Alighting from his car, he found her lying in the road, with a cut on her forehead and with cut or scraped knees. He moved her to the roadside and tried, unsuccessfully, to wave down some cars. Unable to see a telephone box, and thinking it would be unwise to try to put her in his car, he left her by the roadside and went away to get help.

Police officers promptly visited the scene with Goodenough. (However, from information given to me by Sean Tudor, I understand that it may have been police from Maidstone, not Rochester, who were sent to the scene. If so, perhaps Goodenough returned to it by himself.) They found a rug or blanket that Goodenough had used to cover or wrap around the injured girl (or to pull her to safety – see below), although there was no sign of the girl herself. The search for her was resumed at dawn, but she wasn't found, and extensive enquires drew a blank. Of course, assuming that she was a flesh-and-blood person, she may have got up and left the accident scene at some point after Goodenough went away to alert the police.

Judging from what Ted Wright, a retired police dog-handler, told Sean Tudor, the accident victim had been described as a *young woman*, and Goodenough had supposedly rolled her on to a car rug and used it to pull her to safety (rather than lifting her and carrying her to the roadside, as other reports had suggested). Wright told Tudor that neither the rug nor the grass under it was indented. Wright's dog, Bess, detected a scent on the blanket. It led back towards the road, from where, of course, Goodenough had supposedly moved the accident victim in the first place. Possibly, then, it was Goodenough's own scent.

Chatham Road, Blue Bell Hill – site of the Maidens' encounter. (S. Tudor)

A witch-like figure

The occupants of a car had a frightening experience on BBH around 12.45 a.m. on 6 January 1993 while driving home to Rochester after a night out (pp. 248–254). They were on Chatham Road when a figure moved quickly across the road in front of them, from right to left. Malcolm Maiden, who was doing the driving, slowed down. The figure was wearing a very old-fashioned dress, a tartan shawl and a bonnet with a brim. Mrs Maiden commented to her husband that someone was playing a prank. When the figure was fully illuminated by the car's headlights, it remained hunched over. Then, when the onlookers were alongside the figure, it rounded on the car. Mrs Maiden described the face as 'totally horrific', its worst feature being the mouth, which opened and 'was like an empty black hole'. A hissing sound filled the car, even though the windows were closed. The figure held a spray of twigs, which it raised and shook threateningly. As the car drove away, Mrs Maiden's mother saw the figure start towards the nearside kerb, where it seemed to vanish. Judging from accounts in Sean Tudor's book, other road users have had very similar experiences in the

BBH area.

THE WARMINSTER AREA, WILTSHIRE

Warminster is a town in Wiltshire, southern England. It lies on the western edge of Salisbury Plain. In 1965, the town and surrounding area acquired a reputation for anomalous phenomena. Unusual sounds were heard in the town in late 1964. But within a few months, UFO sightings predominated, or at least received more attention. Strange phenomena, not limited to sounds and UFO sightings, reportedly continued well into the 1970s, although by then, the level of activity was apparently lower than in the earlier years. Expectancy, suggestion, imagination and sleep deprivation may have induced skywatchers to misperceive ordinary aerial objects as UFOs, and it's known that some hoaxes were perpetrated. But it wasn't just 'UFO enthusiasts' who reported unusual phenomena – people going about their normal business also had odd experiences.

A man called Arthur Shuttlewood (1920–96) moved to Warminster in about 1940 and served as a councillor for a period. After a stint with the

Colloway Clump, Warminster. (D. Feast)

Wiltshire Times, he worked for many years as a reporter with the *Warminster Journal*. He was also a local correspondent for national newspapers. He had his first UFO sighting in late September 1965, and subsequently spent much time skywatching on the hills outside the town. He wrote several books on the local phenomena, the first and probably best-known being *The Warminster Mystery*, which was first published in 1967. But the reliability of his reporting has been seriously questioned.[23]

According to *The Warminster Mystery* (p. 167), on 16 December 1965 a witness told Shuttlewood that a grey-clad figure with streaming fair hair had jumped in front of his car near Colloway Clump, a hillside copse to the north of the town. It seems that the incident may have happened that very day, at 7.51 p.m. The driver felt certain that he'd hit a 'suicidal maniac', but when he stopped and ran back, there was nothing to be seen. However, the informant declined to give Shuttlewood his address. But he wasn't the only person to report such an incident. Shuttlewood relates (ibid., p.167) that a man and his wife (unnamed) experienced something similar on 21 December that year at another location in the Warminster area. A long-haired figure rushed from a hedge and threw him- or herself under the couple's car. They felt the wheels bump over the figure, although when the husband stopped and got out to check, he saw no body or bloodstains.

WHITE HILL, NEAR WYE, KENT

On Friday, 6 January 2000, Keith Scales, a 53-year-old coach driver, encountered a colliding apparition at 6.45 a.m. while driving to work. He was on a narrow, twisting road, descending White Hill, 2 miles north-east of Wye, Kent. Rounding a bend, he saw a woman in the middle of the road. He subsequently estimated her age to be 30–35 years. She had shoulder-length blond hair and was wearing a long, dark overcoat. Scales didn't have time to avoid her, and he felt the impact of a collision. She smiled as his car hit her, and she bounced over the bonnet and then disappeared. Unusually for cases of this type, the car did show some damage – a broken offside wing-mirror – although it's possible that the damage had occurred sometime previously and had gone unnoticed. Scales searched, but couldn't find the woman. He phoned the police when he reached his workplace. Two officers searched the scene and nearby woodland, but to no avail. A female passenger on his coach told Scales that the same thing had happened to her. Unbeknown to Scales at the time of his experience, the location had a reputation for being haunted. Colleagues of his speculated that the ghost was that of a woman who'd been murdered there by her husband some years previously.[24]

THE A23 NEAR PYECOMBE, WEST SUSSEX

The A23 connects London and Brighton, although a stretch of it is now a motorway (the M23). The village of Pyecombe is located a few miles north of Brighton and consists of two parts, about half a mile apart: Pyecombe itself and Pyecombe Street. Both of them are adjacent to the A23.

Reports of motorists encountering apparitions on the A23 in this area go back at least to the 1970s. John Rackham mentions several sightings in his book *Brighton Ghosts, Hove Hauntings*, some of them being of the colliding apparition type.[25] He refers, for example, to a report in the Brighton *Evening Argus* on 2 December 1976 concerning a couple called Patrick and June Geary. They were about 10 miles north of Brighton and driving towards London when they saw, from behind, a girl in a white raincoat walking along the central reservation. This was around 8 p.m. on a dark night with heavy rain falling. Patrick Geary thought it strange that she didn't appear to have any hands or feet. Without looking, the figure suddenly stepped into the road. There wasn't time to stop, but Mr Geary instinctively turned on the main beam of his headlights. He's quoted as saying that the figure seemed to glide along the top of his bonnet and then disappear. This couple's experience is also mentioned, very briefly, on page 44 of *Ghosts of Today*, a book by the late Andrew Green. He states that they were so convinced that they'd hit the pedestrian that they risked an accident, by stopping and walking back to try to find the person.

Another report (Rackham doesn't specify its source) concerns three young men who, at the beginning of the 1990s, were driving through the village of Bolney (several miles north of Pyecombe) on the A23, and who decided to call in at the pub there. They were about to turn towards the pub's car park when a woman suddenly appeared before their vehicle. The driver braked hard, but the car seemed to hit her, although no bump was felt. The car skidded a few yards and then hit a low wall. The men were shaken but not injured. They jumped out of the vehicle, but there was no sign of the woman. Rackham states that two people who were outside the pub claimed that they had seen her appear from out of nowhere and then vanish when the car hit her. This apparition had reportedly been seen on previous occasions, and was said to be the ghost of a woman who'd been killed on that stretch of road by a passing vehicle many years before.

GENERAL COMMENTS

It's hard to believe that the apparitions discussed above were manifestations of earthbound spirits, since that would imply that certain stretches of road can act like 'psychic cobwebs', trapping multiple unfortunate souls! And the earthbound spirit theory doesn't explain why so many of these apparitional figures act like 'suicidal maniacs' in the presence of road traffic.

The theatricality of these phenomena suggests to me that they are staged events – maybe orchestrations of our 'collective unconscious' or of a tricksterish higher intelligence. However, it's not clear to me what purpose, if any, lies behind the manifestations. One possibility is that they serve as warnings to drive carefully and thereby avoid accidents. However, leaving aside one case, that of Kevin Whelan on the A15, who admitted that he was maybe going a bit too fast, I'm not aware of any evidence suggesting that the drivers I've mentioned were doing anything unduly risky when they encountered colliding apparitions.

PHANTOM HITCHHIKERS

Understood literally, a hitchhiker is someone who stands at a roadside and tries to solicit a lift in, or on, a passing vehicle by holding up a thumb. However, in the literature on road ghost phenomena, the expression *phantom hitchhiker* is used more loosely. For example, it might be applied to an apparitional figure that's seen *within* a vehicle, irrespective of whether it solicited a lift, was invited in by the driver, entered without invitation, or simply appeared unexpectedly. In one of the cases cited below, from Northumberland, a figure, possibly apparitional, was seen trying to hitch a lift, but then seemed to disappear. I'll count it as a possible phantom hitchhiker incident. I'll also mention cases in which drivers gave lifts to people, dropped them off, and then had a reason to doubt whether the passengers had been flesh–and–blood people.

In his book on phantom hitchhikers, Michael Goss claims that stories about them occur in virtually every country of the world.[1] Some of them may be tales that have been passed from person to person, becoming embellished and distorted along the way. Such rumours are sometimes referred to as *foaf-tales*, 'foaf' being an acronym derived from 'friend of a friend'. The essential idea is that the supposed testimony has come through a chain of people, and may be so contaminated with error or deliberate invention as to be evidentially worthless. However, it would be rash to dismiss the phantom hitchhiker phenomenon in its entirety as an 'urban legend', since there are first-hand accounts on record. Admittedly, first-hand testimony may not always be true, but it's likely to be more accurate than a foaf-tale.

A dictionary might define *folklore* as the traditional beliefs and stories of a group of people, or the study of such matters. However, words have the meanings we give them, and are often ambiguous. That's the case with *folklore*, since in the first of the aforementioned senses, a speaker or writer's intention might be to leave open the possibility that there's some historical truth in the folk tale that he or she is mentioning. Other speakers or writers, however, might use the word more restrictively, to refer to stories that – in their view – *aren't* historically true ('The Loch Ness Monster? Forget it, mate – it's just folklore!').

In his analysis of the evidence for phantom hitchhikers, Michael Goss uses *folklore* in this more restrictive sense. He speaks of 'folklore motifs' – recurrent patterns occurring in folk tales. In the ghost stories of folklore and fictional writing, a ghost is generally portrayed as the spirit of a known person, and the tale is likely to have a neat ending that provides the reader or listener with an explanation of the events. For example, a phantom hitchhiker story adhering to a folklore motif might go as follows: A young woman solicits a lift from a passing male driver. She gives him the address of where she wants to be taken, and she's quite talkative. But at some point in the journey, the driver discovers that he's alone in his vehicle, although the woman's scarf has been left behind. The driver calls at the address given, and discovers that the young woman had been killed in an accident on the stretch of road where he picked her up, and that it's now the anniversary of her death.

From Goss's perspective, the more closely an allegedly true phantom hitchhiker story adheres to a folklore motif, the more likely it is to be fictitious. I think he's probably right.

A ROADSIDE FIGURE IN NORTHUMBERLAND

A *Mail Online* article of 10 August 2015 reports an incident that had allegedly occurred during the previous week, on the A696 near Belsay, Northumberland.[2] A slightly different version is given in a *Mirror* article of 7 August 2015.[3]

Radio presenters Chris Felton and Rob Davies were travelling at night along the road, with Felton doing the driving. They noticed a figure by the roadside, completely dressed in beige, apparently trying to hitch a lift.

Felton and Davies were travelling at 60mph at that point and couldn't stop in time to pick up the hitchhiker. Felton turned their vehicle round, and they went back to find the person, even though they both felt that there'd been something odd about the figure. They even joked that it might have been a phantom hitchhiker. They eventually saw the figure again. It was dressed in what Davies described as 'RAF gear' and was holding what looked like a helmet or bag under its arm. By that time, Davies had started filming with his iPhone. A short, but not very clear, video sequence can be seen via the *Mail Online* article, but I don't know whether it's what Davies filmed at the time or a reconstruction. Felton slowed down and turned his vehicle round. But there was now no sign of the hitchhiker, although it was only seconds since they'd last seen the figure. Researching online, they discovered that a trainee RAF pilot, Sergeant John Knight, had been killed in a Spitfire crash in July 1943 at nearby Middlepart Farm (or Middleton Farm, according to the *Mirror* article).

It is very speculative to link this alleged sighting with a pilot's death in 1943. The hitchhiker may have been a flesh-and-blood person who chose to slip away into the darkness, perhaps worried about why a car that had passed on that lonely stretch of road had come back. An anomalous feature of the video clip is that the hitchhiker's left arm seems to be extended, as if he or she were trying to get a lift from someone travelling on his or her side of the road. But the video sequence doesn't appear to show an approaching vehicle. At that point, of course, Felton and Davies were travelling in the opposite direction – not the one in which the hitchhiker apparently wanted to go.

CASES FROM WEST LANCASHIRE

As previously noted, Rob Gandy has received reports of motorists having ghostly experiences on, or near, Halsall Moss in West Lancashire.[4] Four of these (labelled as Cases 1, 3, 4 and 5 below) involve first-hand accounts of the phantom hitchhiker type, and one (Case 2) involves a brief, second-hand story of the same type. (I'm using 'first-hand' and 'second-hand' in relation to Rob Gandy, who received the stories. A story told to him by the witness him- or herself would qualify as a first-hand account, whereas an account relayed by an intermediary would be second-hand.)

Case 1

In the late 1980s, Bill (pseudonym), one of Rob Gandy's work colleagues, described an experience that he'd had one night in February or March 1965 while driving along Gregory Lane towards Ormskirk. As he neared a bridge over a disused railway, he looked in his rear-view mirror and saw the figure of a large, elderly man in the back seat. He had a grey/white scarf round his neck, in the style of a cravat. Bill had the impression that the man was wearing a flat cap. Not surprisingly, Bill was frightened. He stopped the car and got out. While exiting the vehicle, he reached for the starting-handle, with a view to defending himself. However, when he looked, there was no one to be seen.

Case 2

Six or seven years after the above-mentioned incident, Bill was at a social event and met a man who reported having had a similar experience at the same spot. So far as I know, Gandy wasn't personally in touch with that witness.

Case 3

A woman reported an experience that she'd had in the autumn of 2004, around 9.30 p.m., while driving home from work on the A570. As she approached a restaurant, she felt that someone else was in the car with her, and as she came up to the bridge over the Leeds–Liverpool Canal, she turned her head and saw a man, wearing a woollen winter coat and a hat, sitting in the front passenger seat. Because the bridge is on a bend, the driver had to return her attention to the road. When she looked again, the figure was gone. Surprisingly, she didn't find the sighting frightening. It wasn't until the next day that it dawned on her how strange the incident had been.

Case 4

A woman, whom Rob Gandy refers to as 'Mrs H', related that she'd had two experiences of seeing a purple/lilac wisp fluttering across St Helens Road (the A570). A third experience occurred on a winter's night in the 1990s when she was driving along Narrow Lane, dropping down to Halsall from Clieves Hill. At a blind junction with Halsall Lane, she stopped to determine whether the road was clear. While bending forward to look, she noticed, over her left shoulder, the misty figure of a large man in the back seat. He seemed to be in his 60s. He was wearing a grey/beige gabardine coat, and had a yellow/beige scarf round his neck, tied like a cravat. As with the witness in Case 3, Mrs H wasn't perturbed by the apparition. Indeed, she was keen to get home quickly, so that she could show her husband the ghost in the car, although the figure had gone by the time she arrived.

Case 5

On a dark evening in 1988, a woman was driving on the B5195 south of Halsall. As she slowed down to take a corner, she had the distinct impression that a man had got into the back seat of her car and was sitting right behind her. Feeling terrified, she avoided looking in her rear-view mirror or turning round to look at him. Although not religious, she repeated the Lord's Prayer, out loud, over and over again, hoping it would protect her. Eventually, she felt that the passenger wouldn't hurt her, and she became a little less afraid. She slowed to a near stop at Downholland Cross – where there's a pub, the Scarisbrick Arms – since she was about to make a left turn at the crossroads. At that point, the phantom passenger exited the car. The witness caught a glimpse of the figure, which seemed to be that of an agile, strong man, neither old nor young, but of a mature age. He was wearing what appeared to be a leather skirt or apron. The informant added that the car door didn't physically open when the figure left her vehicle.

Comments

In all five of these cases, the ghostly figure seems to have been male, and there are similarities between some of the descriptions (e.g. in terms of the estimated age of the apparitional person). But the sighting reports are too sketchy to tell us whether everyone saw the same figure, albeit differently attired. It would be interesting to know whether, prior to their experiences, the informants had been aware of reports of people having road ghost experiences in the area.

I noted at the beginning of this chapter that the expression 'phantom hitchhiker' is used rather loosely. In none of these cases from West Lancashire did the phantom figure solicit a lift, and there was no conversation between the drivers and their unbidden guests. Arguably, the fact that the apparitions didn't speak adds to the credibility of the reports, since phantom figures are seldom talkative.

Rob Gandy's 2015 article in *Fortean Times* briefly mentions a couple of items posted to an Internet forum entitled 'Haunted roads in Southport and west Lancashire'.[5] One of them referred to a friend of the poster. About 15 years previously, the friend had been driving along Carr Moss Lane, Halsall, late at night, when he felt very cold. Looking in his rear-view mirror, he saw a man, aged about 75–80, in the back seat, dressed in old-fashioned clothes. But when the driver turned to look, the man had gone. The second item wasn't about a 'hitchhiking' phantom, so I shan't go into the details.

It's popularly believed that ghostly events may be linked with tragic deaths, and there have been suggestions that the roads crossing Halsall Moss have seen a higher than expected number of accidents. As mentioned previously, an article by Rob Gandy was published in *The Champion* newspaper, appealing for witness testimony regarding road ghost experiences. Danielle Thompson of Champion Newspapers made a Freedom of Information request to the police in Lancashire regarding accidents in the area in question. The response focused on New Cut Lane and Gregory Lane, which run into each other. Data for a period of 6 years and 10 months suggested that there'd been, on average, around twelve and a half collisions/accidents a year. Gandy feels that this is a little high, but he notes that objective comparisons will be difficult, 'because there are no data on the total volumes of traffic'.

Gandy suggests that given the road conditions in the locality (i.e. sharp bends, lack of lighting and frequent mists), many drivers 'will have a greater sense of awareness and concentration' when driving across Halsall Moss in the dark. He wonders whether anomalous experiences might be prompted by this heightened awareness of environmental features. However, I wonder whether it could be the other way round – that drivers in this flat, drab and often misty terrain might sometimes experience a degree of sensory deprivation, which could be conducive to hallucinations. But I'm not denying that there could be something paranormal about the reported events. If road travellers experience a slightly altered state of consciousness, they might be more prone to psychic influences.

A SHAPE-SHIFTING PASSENGER ON CANNOCK CHASE

In his book about strange phenomena on Cannock Chase, Lee Brickley recounts two incidents that were related to him by a Mr Bird (pseudonym).[6] In about 2006–09, Brickley worked night shifts for a food distribution company. Since he finished work 2 hours before the first local bus operated, and because his co-workers couldn't always offer him a lift, he sometimes had to walk home. On a few occasions, Bird noticed Brickley making his way home on foot, and he then started giving him lifts. One day, Brickley observed that Bird seemed troubled, and he asked what was wrong. Bird told him about something that had happened that morning. Driving on Stile Cop Road, near Rugeley, Bird saw a woman at the roadside. She was staring blankly into the road ahead. Bird turned his car round at the next junction and drove back to her. He asked whether she needed any assistance. She nodded her head and he offered her a lift. Without saying anything, she

Cannock Chase – a paranormal hot spot?

opened one of the rear doors, got into Bird's car and clicked the seat belt into place. Bird chatted away, but the woman, who seemed to be about 25, said nothing. Then, to his horror, Bird noticed, in his rear-view mirror, that the passenger in the back of his car was an old, ugly and evil-looking witch-like figure, dressed in rags. He brought his car to a halt, and turned round to discover that the passenger had vanished.

Subsequently, there was a string of occasions when Bird drove past Brickley without stopping to give him a lift. Eventually, he did stop again, and told Brickley that he'd just seen the woman again on Stile Cop Road, although someone else had stopped to pick her up. Bird had reportedly followed close behind this other vehicle, expecting to see the woman in the back seat vanish. Instead, the vehicle itself, along with the driver and passenger, 'faded to dust' (Brickley's words) before Bird's eyes. From Bird's body language, Brickley concluded that his informant had indeed just been through a traumatic experience. But Bird declined to give Brickley a lift, since he was through with picking up hitchhikers!

Brickley discovered that, in 1984, Cannock Chase Council had opened a cemetery beside Stile Cop Road, because many local burial grounds were at capacity. Its entrance is very close to where Bird claimed to have had his sightings.

Comments

Apparitions are normally thought to be insubstantial things, and it might be thought unlikely that a phantom figure would be able to open the door of a car and engage a seat belt. However, if we assume that the figure of the hitchhiker was a hallucination (albeit of a paranormal nature), it's not a great leap to surmise that the perceived opening and closing of the door, and the sounds of the seat belt being engaged, were also hallucinatory. Another possibility is that there'd actually been no sighting of a phantom figure and a phantom car, but something had edited Bird's memory, leaving him with compelling, but false, recollections of having had those ghostly experiences. This notion of memory tampering gains credibility from the many UFO close encounter cases in which people have reported 'missing time'. Examples will be cited in later chapters.

Bird may have been acting charitably in giving free rides to strangers or relative strangers, but his behaviour carried risks, given the possibility that a passenger might have turned out to be psychopathic or mentally deranged. Therefore, it's conceivable that his ghostly experiences were crafted by his own subconscious mind, or by a protective external intelligence, to deter him from giving such lifts.

A CASE FROM BEDFORDSHIRE

Roy Fulton, a 26-year-old carpet fitter, had a memorable experience on the evening of Friday 12 October 1979, while driving home after a darts match in Leighton Buzzard. It's described in Michael Goss's book *The Evidence for Phantom Hitch Hikers* (p. 11; pp. 90–99). Fulton was on a road near the village of Stanbridge, Bedfordshire, when he saw a male figure on the left, thumbing a lift. Fulton stopped his Mini Van, and the hitchhiker opened the passenger-side door and got in. He was dark-haired and was wearing a dark-coloured jumper, a white-collared shirt and dark-coloured trousers. His face was pale and unusually long. Fulton asked the man where he was going, but the passenger didn't speak – he merely pointed ahead. Although Fulton thought this was slightly unusual, any initial alarm he may have felt was allayed by the thought that the man could have been deaf and dumb. A few minutes later, Fulton turned to offer him a cigarette, but there was no one there. In a subsequent interview with Michael Goss, Fulton estimated that his speed at the time had been 'about 40 minimum'.

The shocked driver called at a bar and ordered a large Scotch to calm his nerves. He then went to the police station in Dunstable and reported the incident – mainly in order to learn whether there had been other reports of a similar nature. However, the Dunstable police informed Michael Goss that they weren't aware of any comparable reports. An article about Fulton's experience appeared in the 18 October 1979 edition of the *Dunstable Gazette*, and the *Sunday Express* covered the story three days later. However, Fulton hadn't sought out the press, looking for publicity – the story had come to the attention of Anne Court, the author of the *Dunstable Gazette* article, through the husband of a friend of Fulton's wife. Goss explains that Court checked the issues of the paper for the weeks following the publication of her piece, to see whether people had written in to report similar experiences. But no one had. Possibly, then, Fulton's experience was a 'one-off' rather than a manifestation of a local haunting.

Comments

Fulton's recollection was that the figure had opened the door of his van, activating the interior lighting in the process. However, one could argue along the lines mentioned above in respect of the Cannock Chase case: if we assume that the figure of the hitchhiker was a hallucination, it's not unreasonable to infer that the perceived opening and closing of the door, and the activation of the lighting, were also hallucinatory. Again, though, another possibility is that there'd been no encounter with a phantom hitchhiker at all, but something had edited Fulton's memory, leaving him with a compelling, but false, recollection of having given a lift to a ghostly figure.

BLUE BELL HILL

The previous chapter cited encounters with colliding apparitions in the Blue Bell Hill area of north Kent. The area has also been the setting for reported phantom hitchhiker incidents, although some of the stories sound more like fanciful folklore than factual reports. Michael Goss's book refers to an article that appeared in the 10 September 1968 edition of *The Gazette*, which he describes as 'Mid-Kent's picture paper' (p. 102). The piece referred to incidents in which motorists had given a lift to an unidentified girl who had been waiting on Blue Bell Hill, near the Lower Bell pub. During these alleged encounters, she would chat all the way to Maidstone, but then vanish in the vicinity of Week Street, a busy shopping thoroughfare.[7]

Accounts gathered by Tom Harber

The aforementioned article in *The Gazette* referred to a Tom Harber, a blind switchboard operator at a hospital in Barming, who'd been trying to contact witnesses. He'd reportedly received eighty or ninety calls concerning local ghosts and related matters, thirty of which were about the BBH hitchhiker, although none of the callers was a first-hand witness.[8] Michael Goss had telephone conversations and a face-to-face meeting with Harber, who explained that he'd eventually traced and interviewed twelve people who claimed to have encountered the ghostly hitchhiker. (Since two of the incidents involved more than one witness, Harber's case material may have related to fewer than twelve separate incidents.) Goss notes that all of the encounters 'occurred at 11 p.m.' (p. 104), which presumably means that they all *began* at 11 p.m.[9] All of the witnesses assumed that the young woman was a real person – at least, initially. She reportedly said that she was due to be married the next day. The only divergent feature was that, in a few instances, the young woman wanted to go to Chatham rather than Maidstone. The witness in Harber's first case (from 1966) allegedly called at an address the young woman had given, concerned for her well-being, and was told that she'd been killed in a car crash exactly a year before he met the hitchhiker.

These alleged witness reports have a strong folklore flavour, and Goss contends that they must remain articles of faith for those disposed to accept them, and as 'inadmissibly uncorroborative matter' for those who aren't (p. 104). And he adds that the tales never appeared in print. For his part, Harber related the encounters to a tragic vehicle collision on BBH, which occurred on 19 November 1965, involving a Mark 1 Ford Cortina containing four young women, and a Jaguar containing two people. Three of the women in the Cortina were fatally injured, including the 24-year-old driver, who was due to be married the next day.[10] She died in West Kent Hospital, Maidstone, five days after the accident.

If credence is given to Harber's cases, it would seem that the young woman featuring in them was the ghost of the bride-to-be, although Goss (p. 108) explains that, in other accounts, the ghost is identified with one of her companions. However, in his recently published book, *The Ghosts of Blue Bell Hill & other Road Ghosts*, Sean Tudor notes that there are difficulties in linking the ghostly encounters on BBH with the 1965 crash. For example, in November 1993 he interviewed a man named Jack Woodger, who had encountered a possible phantom hitchhiker as early as 1934, long before the 1965 accident (pp. 223–225). On the night in question, Woodger was riding a motorcycle when he saw a girl standing in the middle of the road outside the Lower Bell pub on BBH. She said that she had to go to Burham, a nearby village. He took her there, dropping her off in Church Street. Turning his motorbike round for the return journey, he looked back to see that she'd vanished.

James Skene's experience

Tudor's book refers to a James Skene, who told him about an experience that he'd had one night in about 1971 (pp. 218–221). He was driving on the A229, construction of which was still underway, somewhere in the vicinity of the Lower Bell pub on BBH. A woman appeared in his path, and he swerved around her. He stopped and pushed open his passenger door, intending to chide her for nearly causing an accident. But before he'd spoken, she got into his car! She appeared to be in her 20s, and asked to be taken to Chatham. Skene was heading the other way – to Maidstone – but he went out of his way and drove her to Chatham. In describing the incident to Sean Tudor, he couldn't recall whether the woman opened the door to let herself out. After she exited the vehicle, he reversed round a corner in order to turn his car round. While doing so, he noticed that the woman had disappeared. He thought this was odd, but it was only when he heard about Maurice Goodenough's story (discussed in the previous chapter) that he began to ponder the incident.

Richard Studholme's story

A short article in the 9 May 1975 issue of the now defunct magazine *Reveille* described a strange experience that a 19-year-old guitarist, Richard Studholme (misspelt as 'Stodholme' in the article), had supposedly had, beginning just after midnight on an unspecified date. He'd allegedly stopped on Blue Bell Hill (wrongly named as 'Blueberry Hill' in the article) to give a lift to a 'girl' (unfortunately, the article gave no estimate of her age). She asked Studholme to drop her off in West Kingsdown, after which she wanted him to call on her parents, in Swanley, to explain that he'd given her a lift and that she was well! When Studholme arrived at the address he'd been given, a bereaved father told him that, 2 years previously, his daughter had been killed at the very spot where the hitchhiker had been picked up. Studholme initially assumed that he'd been the victim of a hoax, even though the hitchhiker's clothing resembled what the daughter had been wearing on the night she was killed. But after reading of other strange happenings at the spot where he'd picked up the girl, he wondered whether he'd encountered a phantom hitchhiker.

In his book, Sean Tudor reports that in 1994 he conducted a brief telephone interview with Studholme, who estimated that the hitchhiker encounter had occurred around 1973. If so, it would have happened when he was about 22 – not 19, as stated in the *Reveille* article.[11] His recollection of the incident differed, in significant respects, from its portrayal in the magazine. He told Tudor that the girl had asked to be dropped off at the top of BBH (not in West Kingsdown), and that the address that he was asked to call at was in the Walderslade area (not Swanley). He said that he still thought that the hitchhiker had been a hoaxer. Tudor (p. 161) explains that the 5 November 1971 edition of the *Kent Messenger* reported that a 21-year-old woman had died in hospital after a three-car pile-up near the foot of BBH. But she was apparently from Frindsbury, not Walderslade. All told, then, it's hard to come to firm conclusions about Studholme's account.

Comments

The above should be regarded as illustrative reports, not an exhaustive list. Sean Tudor's book contains additional accounts of phantom hitchhiker encounters on BBH, and also mentions sightings of apparitions of a more passive character (i.e. phantoms that didn't try to solicit lifts or otherwise interact with the witnesses). All told, the area appears to have generated a considerable number of reports of ghostly activity.

THE A38, SOMERSET

For this section, I've drawn on Michael Goss's book (pp. 82–86) and Sean Tudor's website.[12] There are several stories, which may all relate to the same apparitional figure, that of a man. With most of the witnesses, the figure simply acted as an apparition of the colliding type. But with another witness, if his account can be believed, the figure also played the role of a phantom hitchhiker.

In August 1970, a Mrs Karen Swithenbank was driving on the A38 near Heatherton Grange Hotel, south-west of Taunton, when she saw a middle-aged man in a long, grey coat standing in the middle of the road. She swerved to avoid him. She intended to remonstrate with him, but then noticed that he'd vanished. An account of her experience was published, and similar stories were then related by other motorists. They included a motorcyclist who'd fallen off his machine and broken a limb at White Ball, 4 miles west of where Mrs Swithenbank had encountered the troublesome figure.

The publicity about these incidents encouraged a lorry driver called Harold Unsworth to come forward, in 1970, regarding multiple encounters that he'd allegedly had with what may have been the same figure. He'd kept quiet about the matter for 12 years, being fearful of ridicule and reluctant to believe what he'd experienced. The first incident began at 3 a.m., in poor weather. Unsworth was heading back to his depot at Cullompton, Devon. He noticed a bedraggled, middle-aged man in a cream or grey mac waiting, torch in hand, near the Blackbird Inn, a mile west of Heatherton Grange. Feeling sorry for him, Unsworth stopped to give the pedestrian a lift. In a well-educated voice, the man asked to be dropped off at Beam Bridge, by the Holcombe Rogus crossroads. He spent part of the 4-mile journey talking about how many accidents there'd been during the week. Goss (p. 3) states, somewhat vaguely, that the situation was repeated a few days later, and then again after a month. The late hour and bad weather were consistent features. Given the pedestrian's odd behaviour – being on the road in the dead of night, and in pouring rain – and his choice of conversational topics, Unsworth wondered whether the man was mentally defective.

Unsworth encountered the man again in November 1958. As previously, the passenger asked to be taken to Beam Bridge. But when they got there, he asked Unsworth to wait, saying that he needed to collect some cases and then wanted to be taken further along the road. Unsworth allegedly waited 20 minutes, but the man didn't reappear, and so Unsworth resumed his journey. Near a transport café about 3 miles further along the road, he saw a torch being waved. He thought that another motorist might be in trouble, but his headlights then revealed the man in the mac. However, no other vehicle had come along the road in either direction. Unsworth's sense of alarm made him unwilling to pick up the man again. He began to pull out, whereupon the man threw himself in front of the lorry, although there was no sensation of impact. Unsworth braked, brought the vehicle to a halt after a few dozen yards, and jumped from the cab. The man was in the middle of the road, shaking a fist and cursing. Then he turned his back and vanished in an instant.

It seems that the sightings may not have been restricted to the countryside. One evening in 1973, a Mrs Taylor was driving on New Road, Taunton, when she encountered a middle-aged man in a long, grey overcoat standing in the middle of the road, seemingly looking at something on the ground. She swerved to avoid him, but when she got out of her car to berate him, he'd vanished.

Assuming that the same figure has featured in all the incidents, this appears to be a long-running road haunting. As recently as December 1991, there was an incident on the A38 near the village of Rumwell. Rounding a bend, a female motorist saw a man in a grey raincoat in the middle of the road, flashing a torch at her. After swerving to avoid him, she ended up in a ditch. 'Fuming', she got out of her vehicle, intending to remonstrate with him, but he'd disappeared.

Comments

The mysterious man in Unsworth's story started out as a phantom hitchhiker and then, during the final encounter, became a colliding apparition, although his apparitional status only became evident during that last incident. But there are things about the account that strain my credulity, even leaving aside the possible paranormal aspects. According to Goss (p. 83), Unsworth was relieved to part company with the strange man after their first meeting. If so, why did he stop on subsequent occasions to give the creepy pedestrian a lift? And regarding the November 1958 episode, there's the odd matter of what happened when Unsworth and the passenger reached Beam Bridge. As noted, Unsworth allegedly waited in vain for *20 minutes* for the man to return to the lorry with cases. Yet Unsworth and the pedestrian weren't relatives, friends or colleagues; and presumably Unsworth had a job to do (since he was driving a lorry). If the story is true, he must have been a very patient man!

Regarding the supposedly paranormal aspects, it's noteworthy that the pedestrian not only conversed with Unsworth, but did so on several occasions. However, apparitions aren't usually great talkers. In fact, they typically say nothing, and their appearances tend to be brief. In Unsworth's story, the ghostly figure seemed to take umbrage at not being given a lift near the transport café. But that sounds like something from fiction or folklore – where ghosts might well display anger or act vengefully towards people who have annoyed them. In short, I have doubts about the historical accuracy of Unsworth's story.

5

ALIEN BIG CATS

People on safari in Kenya or Tanzania might expect to see native lions and cheetahs, and travellers exploring the rugged wilds of North America might not be surprised to see pumas (mountain lions). Conversely, road users in the UK might be shocked and surprised to encounter big cats. Yet numerous sightings have been reported over the years, and in some cases they've been backed up by physical evidence. Writing in the 1980s, Janet and Colin Bord remarked that on the basis of the sheer number of reports over the preceding 25 years, the British big cat must rank as the greatest mystery.[1] These out-of-place felines – whether flesh-and-blood animals or something stranger – have come to be known as *alien* (or *anomalous*) *big cats* (ABCs). The adjective 'alien' in this context doesn't, of course, mean extraterrestrial – it's simply a shorthand way of saying that the type of creature seen isn't one that would be expected to be found in the relevant area in *modern* times. I emphasise 'modern', because – as Merrily Harpur points out in her interesting book on ABCs – various types of big cat were once native to this country.[2]

Harpur (p. 51) notes that in the early 1980s, sightings of black ABCs started to predominate over those involving tawny ones. Witnesses have often described the creatures they've seen as 'black panthers'. However, as Harpur explains (p. 9), leopards and jaguars are the only big cats that have a melanistic (black) form, although it's not common. Therefore, if ABCs are flesh-and-blood creatures, it's puzzling that so many of them seem to be black. Of course, it's possible that, in some cases, witnesses have been mistaken about the colour of the creatures – for example, where the sightings were fleeting or where the lighting wasn't very good. And if media reports have instilled the notion of 'black panthers' in the public consciousness, that could presumably influence witnesses' interpretation of what they've seen.

More generally, it's probable that many sightings of 'big cats' are misidentifications of conventional animals. That may have been the case with a 'lioness' that was spotted and photographed during the evening of 26 August 2012 by two couples who were spending the Bank Holiday weekend in caravans at Earls Hall Farm in St Osyth, about 5 miles west of Clacton-on-Sea, Essex. They notified the police and a search ensued, involving about thirty officers, including a firearms team, and a couple of helicopters equipped with thermal imaging equipment. Zoo staff with tranquilliser guns participated. Additional members of the public saw the creature, although they didn't all agree that it was a lion or lioness. Gill Atkin felt that its ears were too pointed for it to be a lion. The search was unsuccessful and was called off shortly before 3 p.m. the next day. The police deemed that what had been seen the previous day was a large domestic cat or a wildcat. One of the staff at Colchester Zoo analysed the photographs, but described them as being of too poor a quality for positive identification. A colleague of his thought that the animal was a large dog, while Ginny Murphy, a local resident, thought that it was 'Teddy Bear', her Maine Coon cat.[3]

In line with the main theme of this book, the cases cited in this chapter will largely relate to road users. The majority of ABC sightings are on the road, but they've been seen in other settings – for example, by people looking out from their homes, and by walkers in the countryside.

EXAMPLES

On 18 July 1963, David Beck was driving through Shooters Hill in south-east London when he spotted a large animal, which he assumed was an injured dog, lying by the roadside. He approached it, and noticed that it was actually a big cat. It had a long tail that curved upwards. The creature ran off into a wood. Police officers in a patrol car had a surprise that very night: what was described as a large, golden animal jumped over the bonnet of their vehicle. Checks were made, but zoos and circuses indicated that none of their animals was missing. A large-scale search ensued, involving police, soldiers, ambulance men and officials from the RSPCA. Apart from some tracks, nothing was found. The paw marks were about 7 inches across, and hence of the size normally associated with lions or tigers. However, they included claw impressions, which is a characteristic of cheetah paw prints, not those of a lion or tiger.[4]

In an article about strange creatures seen in Rendlesham Forest, Suffolk, Nick Redfern refers to a motorist called Jimmy Freeman. He told Redfern that he was driving past Rendlesham Forest one dark, cloudy and slightly misty night in the 1970s when, in his full beam, he saw something large and shadowy charging across the road in front of him. He was convinced that it was a huge black cat.[5]

At 1.30 a.m. on 9 June 1981, a chiropodist named Adrian Grier was driving in Bedfordshire when he saw what looked like a Great Dane in his headlights. However, as he got nearer, it appeared to be a lioness. When he was 10 yards from it, it trotted away and entered a field. He estimated that its length was 6ft and that its height was more than 3½ feet. A report about the sighting appeared in the press, and other witnesses came forward, including a pedestrian who'd allegedly been followed one night in Luton by the largest 'dog' he had ever seen. He identified it as a dog because he couldn't think what else it might have been.[6]

In December 1991, two women and their children encountered an ABC while driving along a lane in Somerset. A black creature with massive teeth threw itself against the side of the vehicle and the children started screaming. According to Lynn Wardell, one of the women, it was a big animal, like a panther or puma. The driver, Susan Stritch, stopped the car, to see whether she had killed it, whereupon it leapt into a clump of bushes. She explained that there was no blood, although the collision had left a huge dent in the car.[7] Leaving aside the damage to the car, this incident is reminiscent of the colliding apparitions discussed in Chapter 3 of this book. Harpur (p. 181) mentions three similar cases from the archive of the Ayrshire-based researcher Mark Fraser. Two of the encounters occurred very close to each other on the same stretch of road, although they involved differently coloured ABCs – one was of a light tan colour; the other was jet-black.

On a summer's evening in the 1990s, Merrily Harpur was driving in Gloucestershire when, about 80 yards ahead, a black, smooth-coated animal loped across the lane she was on and vaulted up a steep bank. Its head had a feline profile. Harpur noticed that it had a long, looped tail. Although its height was that of a roe deer, the creature was longer. This may have been a sighting of what local newspapers had dubbed the 'Beast of Gloucester'.[8]

According to reports, various types of out-of-place animal have been seen on Cannock Chase over the years. During a visit in April 2008, I spoke to a woman who was walking her dogs. She told me of an occasion, some 10 years previously, when she'd seen what she took to be a big cat while she was driving in the area. It crossed a road and jumped over a hedge.

On a bright morning in May 2001, Kim Welsh and her 12-year-old daughter were travelling by car near Ringwood, Hampshire, when a large, jet-black cat emerged from a hedge and stood in the middle of the lane. Welsh braked, but the cat didn't move. Therefore, Welsh brought the car to a halt. The creature was just feet from the bonnet. Its length seemed to equal or exceed the width of the Nissan Serena car, which was just over five and a half feet wide. The cat had huge paws and a tail that was looped up at the end. Welsh described its head as domed and 'panther-like', with amber eyes. After staring at the occupants of the car for an estimated 30 seconds, the creature sauntered to the right and disappeared into a hedge.[9]

ARE ALIEN BIG CATS NORMAL, FLESH-AND-BLOOD CREATURES?

A frequently aired suggestion is that the Dangerous Wild Animals Act of 1976 induced many big cat owners to release their animals into the countryside, rather than pay for the expensive licences stipulated by the Act. However, even if that's the case, it constitutes only a partial explanation of the ABC phenomenon, since there were many reports prior to 1976.

Over several months in 1980, numerous sheep and deer were killed by an unknown predator on the Cannich Estate in the Scottish Highlands. A local farmer, Ted Noble, had seen a creature resembling a lioness in the hills. He made a cage-trap and baited it with a sheep's head. On 29 October of that year, he and his son found a female puma in the trap. She was given a new home at the Kincraig Wildlife Park near Aviemore, and became known as Felicity. She seemed to settle in well, and the director of the wildlife park speculated that she was used to captivity and had been released into the wild only days or hours before being caught. However, droppings obtained about one and a half days after she was captured contained deer, sheep and rabbit remains, which suggested that she'd been a successful predator in the wild. Ted

Noble received a letter from a David Carter, who purported to be a prison inmate at Winchester in southern England. He alleged that he'd released two pumas in the Highlands in 1979. They'd supposedly been passed on to him by a friend who could no longer keep them, because he was moving back to Germany. Carter referred to the pumas as 'cubs', but a vet who examined Felicity shortly after her capture thought that she was about 6 years old.[10]

Merrily Harpur notes (p. 37) that by being easily captured, Felicity demonstrated what should have been the fate of hundreds of other released big cats – had they existed. However, according to Harpur, Felicity remains the only specimen. By the same token, in Chapter 5 of her book, she rejects the 'escapes theory' – the notion that the ABC phenomenon can be accounted for in terms of big cats escaping from circuses, zoos and the like. She explains, for example, that escaped big cats are usually recaptured without great difficulty. She notes (p. 44) that the only recorded case of one surviving for a protracted period in the wild was that of a clouded leopard that got out of Howlett's Park in Canterbury and was on the loose for 8 months before being shot by a farmer. In Chapter 10 of her book, she also considers the 'hide-out theory', the notion that Britain's ABCs are native species left over from the Ice Age. But as she notes, there are several objections to it. For example, if these creatures have been 'hiding out' for so long, one would expect a good many of them to have been killed or trapped.

There are numerous strands of evidence suggesting that ABCs are physical. For example, dead animals (sheep, deer, etc.) have been found with marks characteristic of big cat attacks, and paw marks are sometimes present at sites where ABCs have been seen. Nevertheless, they are in many ways elusive. In 1983, a large number of sheep were killed on Exmoor in south-west England, and there were sightings of a large, black cat in the area. Over several weeks, Royal Marines, equipped with equipment for seeing and shooting in the dark, staked out the moor at night, but the so-called Beast of Exmoor wasn't killed or captured.

If Britain's ABCs are essentially normal flesh-and-blood big cats, people would be expected to come across their skeletal remains from time to time. However, there seems to be a dearth of such evidence. Harpur (pp. 76–77) refers to the discovery of a big cat's skull in January 1988 near Lustleigh, Devon. It was found under the remnants of a plastic bag, which contained a tooth. The obvious inference is that the remains had been dumped. Harpur (p. 75) notes that the front portion of a big cat's skull was found on Exmoor in 1993, but there were indications that it had been a mounted trophy. In

1995, a large feline skull was found in the River Fowey on Bodmin Moor, Cornwall, but was eventually deemed to be from a young male leopard that had died abroad. The skull had probably been a hunting trophy, and may have been placed on the moor as a hoax (Harpur, pp. 75–76). An article in the *Birmingham Post* (29 March 2006) referred to a man – who didn't want to be named – who had allegedly photographed the remains of what he believed was a big cat while out walking on Cannock Chase, Staffordshire, that week. According to the article, the pictures showed a skull that was too large to be that of a domestic animal. The man was quoted as saying that the fangs were 'enormous' and definitely not those of a dog or fox. Nearby, there were reportedly a few other bones, and a trap, secured to a tree, with a bone caught in it. However, since the man was anonymous and there was no mention of the items having been examined by experts, the status of this report is uncertain.

Given their habit of crossing roads, we might have expected a fair number of road kills involving ABCs. Harpur (pp. 71–74) mentions stories of road users seeing bodies of what appeared to be big cats, but with the carcasses then seemingly vanishing, which – in her view – gives a whiff of 'urban legend' to the roadside corpse.

ABCs that have been shot also have a habit of disappearing. For example, Harpur (pp. 74–75) cites a case from Aberdeenshire in 1995. Stan Windsor, a retired gamekeeper, was minding the farm of a friend who was away on holiday. He shot an ABC from a distance of only 35ft, using both barrels of his shotgun. Its tail flew up over its back and it staggered sideways down a hill. Windsor followed it, expecting to find it dead, but there was no sign of it, and a helicopter search by the police the next day also drew a blank.

LANDSCAPE FEATURES ASSOCIATED WITH ALIEN BIG CATS

As already indicated, the majority of ABC sightings occur on roads. But Harpur (Chapter 12) points out that other landscape features often appear in reports. A disproportionate number of sightings occur close to railway lines. In some cases, ABCs have been seen on the tracks. Of course, in built-up areas, railway embankments might provide food (e.g. rabbits) and shelter for big cats. However, Harpur notes that ABC sightings are just as frequent beside railways in rural areas, where a railway might be the busiest part of the landscape (p. 117). Quarries, tunnels, holes and golf courses also feature disproportionately in ABC reports, according to Harpur. Her impression is that ABCs appear 'at interruptions or changes in an otherwise consistent landscape' (p. 123).

If there is a statistically significant association between these landscape features and ABC encounters, there could be fairly prosaic explanations. For example, ravines and tunnels could provide cover for big cats, and if golf courses are fringed with trees, they could also offer cover. But drawing on the speculations of other writers, Harpur seems to prefer a more mystical interpretation, based on the Chinese philosophical system known as feng shui, in which landscape features are described in terms of *yin* ('female' or 'negative' energy) and *yang* ('male' or 'positive' energy). The latter is supposedly related to pointed mountains or buildings, and to straight lines, whereas yin is deemed to be associated with watery, low-lying areas and places such as hollows, caves and cemeteries. Feng shui aims at harmonising or balancing the yin and yang elements in the environment. Harpur speculates that ABCs are yin creatures and that by appearing in the vicinity of straight railway lines, they balance the yang associated with the latter!

Like Jeremy Harte, whose study of Dorset ghosts was discussed in Chapter 3 of this book, Harpur believes that there may be something special about 'liminal zones' (physical or metaphorical boundary areas). She thinks that there's a particularly strong link between phantom black dogs and liminal places, and that there's also such a connection in some ABC cases. On page 55 of her book, she mentions, for example, the experience of an Anne Coombs, who saw an ABC pass through an archway into a churchyard. However, virtually anywhere could, in one way or another, be construed as 'liminal'. For example, if Coombs had been on her way to the church and had seen the ABC a couple of hundred yards from the building, one could say that she was passing through a liminal zone to get to the church. Indeed, *any* road journey could be deemed as a trip through a liminal zone, because the road, even if very long, comes between the point of departure and the intended destination. Even if a carefully conducted statistical study demonstrated a link between clearly defined 'liminal' places and ABC sightings, it wouldn't tell us *why* liminality is important. Harpur's book doesn't really address this.

THEORIES

From a sceptical point of view, it could be argued that there's no real mystery about supposed ABC incidents, and that sightings of out-of-place big cats in the UK are explicable in terms of misperception, misinterpretation, mass hysteria and hoaxing. Hoaxing could take the form of invented sighting reports, or the fabrication of physical traces.

For those believing that ABC sightings are generated by essentially normal, flesh-and-blood big cats, there are several (not mutually exclusive) possibilities, which have already been touched on: the supposed creatures may have been living on our islands, largely unobserved, for centuries; alternatively, they may be big cats that have been deliberately released from captivity by their owners; or they could be large felines that have somehow escaped from captivity.

Influenced by her brother's interest in the philosophy of the Ancient Greeks, and particularly that of the Neoplatonists, Harpur's preferred theory is of a more paranormal kind. She deems that ABCs are *daimons* (not to be confused with demons): creatures that the Ancient Greeks regarded as being the inhabitants and expression of the *anima mundi* (soul of the world), an intermediate realm between that of the gods and the materiality of Earth and human life. She notes (p. 131) that their characteristics can be contradictory, depending on what their role dictates. Thus, they can be material or immaterial, benign or malevolent, and inspiring or indifferent to people. From this perspective, all sorts of mysterious and paranormal entities could be described as daimons (e.g. fairies, small black-eyed aliens, phantom hitchhikers and bigfoot). In essence, Harpur seems to be using the word 'daimons' for what others describe as 'interdimensional' beings – entities that are able to enter our world from some sort of parallel world or alternative reality.

But there are other possibilities. In Chapter 1, I mentioned the notion that people's minds can interact at a subconscious level and generate paranormal phenomena, perhaps in response to a collective wish for there to be evidence of UFOs, ghosts and suchlike. I called this the 'psychic internet theory'. It can be applied to ABCs. From its perspective, ABCs could be construed as *tulpas* (materialised thought-forms). By having a physical aspect – albeit, perhaps, only transitory – they would be able to affect the environment and leave traces.

Another possibility is that ABC manifestations, along with a wide range of other phenomena, are theatrical displays orchestrated by a higher intelligence. From this perspective, the entity or object encountered is a temporary 'stage prop' – a creation of the moment, with no enduring existence and no self-consciousness, rather like a figure in a computer-generated animation. We might surmise that the orchestrating intelligence has a variety of 'tools' at its disposal. In some instances (e.g. involving colliding apparitions) the effects might be brought about by inducing people to experience hallucinations, whereas in other cases (e.g. ABC manifestations) there might be transient materialisations, thereby allowing physical effects to occur.

PHANTOM BLACK DOGS

Stories about phantom dogs abound in British folklore, and also in reports that probably have a factual basis. These apparitional dogs are usually black, but other colours are sometimes reported. The manifestations could reflect just one entity, something that's able to appear in different places and maybe different forms. Or perhaps we're dealing with multiple entities. Alternatively, these could be mere appearances, orchestrated for effect or some other purpose. At any rate, depending on the area, black dogs have been given different names – for example, Black Shuck (in East Anglia), Trash (in Lancashire) and Barghest (in the Yorkshire Dales).

According to legend, there were dramatic sightings of a black dog at two Suffolk churches – St Mary's in Bungay, and Holy Trinity in Blythburgh – during a severe thunderstorm on Sunday, 4 August 1577. The creature supposedly killed people at both sites. But according to parapsychologist Simon Sherwood, historical records pertaining to the two churches *don't* mention a fearsome dog.[1] Nevertheless, the fabled creature has become Bungay's symbol. It appears on the town's coat of arms, and a weathervane in Bungay depicts the legendary dog. It also gets a mention by The Darkness, a British rock band – the opening track of their successful debut album of 2003, *Permission to Land*, is 'Black Shuck'.

EXAMPLES

Greta Shirt had an encounter in 1930 while heading home around 8 p.m. on a lonely lane near Upper Booth in Derbyshire. In the moonlight, she saw a large, black dog, which passed close to her. She put out a hand to stroke it, but felt nothing beneath her fingers. The dog confirmed its ghostly status by passing through the close, criss-cross wires of a fence. When Shirt arrived home and told her father what had happened, he revealed that he'd also seen the dog.[2]

Ernest Whiteland had an encounter in Ditchingham, Norfolk, in 1938, while walking home after spending the evening with friends. He saw a black object, about 75 yards away, approaching him. As it got nearer, he could see that it was a large, black dog. He moved to the middle of the road to let it pass, but it vanished when it got level with him. He looked around, but there was no sign of it, and when he looked over a hedge, expecting to see or hear it in a meadow, there was no indication of it. He later learned that the area was said to be haunted by Black Shuck.[3]

On 19 April 1972, coastguard Graham Grant was on duty at the Gorleston rescue HQ in Norfolk. At daybreak, around 4.45 a.m., he was looking north when he spotted a large, black, hound-type dog on the beach about a quarter of a mile away. It was running and stopping, as if looking for someone. Grant watched it for one or two minutes and it then disappeared before his eyes. At that point, he'd never heard of Black Shuck.[4]

Grant's experience wasn't entirely typical, because phantom black dogs normally appear much closer to witnesses. An even more unusual incident was described to Janet and Colin Bord in correspondence from a Mr H. Holmes. His experience reportedly occurred late at night in 1931, and involved multiple dogs. He was cycling home from a church service in Swaledale, North Yorkshire, and reached Barton Quarry. Suddenly, he noticed a dog-like figure. He dismounted from his bicycle and sat down. It seemed to be a large, grey dog with flashing eyes and also a tongue that was flashing and frothing. A black dog then appeared, running along about 5 yards from the first one. After twenty dogs had passed, Homes dived at one, thinking he would be able to make some money by selling it at a market! However, he ended up in a bed of nettles. He related that the dogs resembled Old English sheepdogs, but were much larger, about a metre in height, with shaggy coats and big heads. They made no noise. He didn't find the experience frightening.[5]

Although it didn't happen on a road, it may be worth mentioning an experience reported by Simon Sherwood, since it shows that apparitional black creatures can appear within buildings. It was around 1974, and Sherwood was aged about 4 at the time. He'd been in bed for a couple of hours when he woke to hear the patter of feet. He looked up, thinking that it was his dog. But to his terror, he saw a massive black animal galloping along the landing towards his bedroom. He tried to scream, but was unable to. The creature had bright yellow eyes, which were as big as saucers. When it reached his bedroom door, it vanished. Since Sherwood had just woken up, his experience may be explicable – as he acknowledges – in terms of hypnopompic imagery (vivid imagery experienced while emerging from sleep) and temporary sleep paralysis.[6] Obviously, though, these conditions don't apply to the black dog experiences of pedestrians and motorists.

PHANTOM BLACK DOGS COMPARED WITH ALIEN BIG CATS

Phantom dogs and ABCs have a habit of frequenting roads, and the majority – from both categories – are black (although that hasn't always been the case with ABCs). However, as Merrily Harpur observes in Chapter 6 of her book *Mystery Big Cats*, there are many differences between phantom black dogs and ABCs. The following are some of them:

Phantom black dogs	ABCs
They're generally seen at night or in twilight.	They're often seen in bright daylight.
Their coats are generally shaggy or woolly.	Their fur tends to be sleek and glossy.
They often appear very close to witnesses.	They usually keep a distance.
Their eyes are often red and/or glowing.	Their eyes are usually green or amber.
They're often seen, repeatedly, on the same stretch of road.	Their appearances are unpredictable and shortlived.
They often disappear into thin air.	They often disappear into hedges.
They're usually solitary.	They're sometimes seen with other ABCs, not necessarily of the same type.
They display a limited range of behaviour.	They display a wide range of behaviour.
They leave no physical traces.	They often leave physical traces.

OMENS OF DEATH

If the reports can be believed, and depending on how they're interpreted, it seems that encounters with phantom dogs are occasionally omens of death for the witnesses themselves or people they know. However, a problem with such accounts is that if the death occurs at some point after the sighting, it's hard to know whether there's any real connection. After all, unexpected deaths (from sudden illnesses, accidents, etc.) are sadly commonplace. The following case illustrates this difficulty.

A married couple were driving home on a misty evening in early January 1978. As they were going downhill, in the direction of Exford, Somerset, they saw a strange dog approaching them on the right-hand side of the road. It was of an Alsatian type, with long, dirty, white hair, which stood up in what looked like frozen spikes. It seemed almost transparent and had red, glowing eyes, although that may have been an illusion created by the car's headlights. Its head was lowered and it looked baleful. It stared sideways at the couple in the car. The wife, who related the incident to Janet and Colin Bord in 1983, explained that her husband had died in horrible circumstances later in 1978, and that her life had changed drastically and unpleasantly. But the report doesn't specify the precise date of the husband's death. Therefore, it's possible that it occurred months after the sighting.[7]

Of course, if the sighting of a phantom dog actually coincides with the death of someone known to the witness, there's a stronger case for thinking that it was an omen. (NB: I'm using the word 'omen' rather loosely here, since – understood literally – it is a portent of something to come, not a symbol or marker of a concurrent event.) Again, though, caution is warranted, because remarkable coincidences will occur occasionally, purely by chance.

The Bords cite a case from Norfolk, in 1930, in which a man had an encounter with a phantom black dog on the road near a church. He subsequently learned that his brother had died at the time of the sighting.[8] This story is reminiscent of a case, from 1981, mentioned by Nigel Mortimer.[9] It involved a Steve Hart, who was travelling home to Leeds on public transport. Close to Addingham in West Yorkshire, he saw a large ball of orange light hanging in the sky over the moorland. He was suddenly overcome by a feeling of intense sorrow and dread, which persisted for as long as he had the object in sight. When he arrived home, he learned that his grandmother had died during the time of his sighting.

Comments

It could be argued that the black dog seen near the church in Norfolk and the ball of orange light seen in West Yorkshire were hallucinatory experiences related to information that the percipients had somehow picked up, by ESP, regarding the death, or imminent death, of a close relative. In the Norfolk case, the hallucination may have taken the form of a black dog because such entities are reputed to be omens of death, although I don't know whether the witness took it to be such at the time. Regarding the West Yorkshire case, it's puzzling that Steve Hart should have seen a ball of orange light – although it's conceivable that for him, or more generally in his family or local community, such a vision would symbolise a death. At any rate, it's not clear what purpose – if any – such an experience would have. In Steve Hart's case, for example, it's hard to see how the sense of intense sorrow and dread evoked by seeing the ball of light served any useful purpose – it probably just added to the unhappiness that he was going to experience anyway on learning of his grandmother's death.

In respect of Black Shuck, or what she simply calls 'Shuck', folklorist Jennifer Westwood questions the idea that encounters with it tend to be omens of death. Citing a publication by Christopher Reeve (which I haven't seen myself),[10] she notes that out of seventy-four sightings compiled from eyewitnesses in 1977, only seventeen could be connected with death or misfortune.[11]

PHANTOM DOGS AS PROTECTORS

Judging from some accounts, apparitional dogs can be protective or even life-saving. Jennifer Westwood (pp. 57–58) quotes a passage from Christopher Reeve's book pertaining to the experience of a Mr E. Ramsey of Bawburgh, Norfolk. He was cycling home on a moonlit night. As he approached the village, he saw the biggest hound that he'd ever seen. It was sitting by a signpost and had eyes that shone like coals of fire. When he was half a mile further along the road, Ramsey heard the dog coming up behind him. He feared that it was going to attack him. Instead, it passed close by him, whereupon he could smell its rankness. It then stopped in the middle of the road, on the fringe of a copse, and faced him. It looked aggressive, so Ramsey stopped by a hedge, hoping that someone would come along to help him. Just then, there was the roar of a vehicle coming along the road through the copse. The vehicle emerged with no lights, veering from side to side. The dog was in its path and was seemingly hit by it. The vehicle came so close to Ramsey that he fell into the hedge with his cycle on top of him. After picking himself up, he was amazed to see the dog still standing where it had been. It turned and then simply vanished.

Alan Murdie reports that in 2003, a woman informed him of an occasion, in 1996, when a spectral black dog had appeared near her on a footpath in woodland at Manningtree, Essex. It deterred unwelcome attention from local vagrants.[12] Jeremy Harte quotes a story (from Lincolnshire, it seems) reported by the folklorist Ethel Rudkin. A woman was returning home on foot and noticed that a very large dog was walking behind her. Eventually, she passed some Irish labourers and heard them say what they would have done to her (rape?) if the dog hadn't been with her. When she got home, she called her husband to come and see the dog, but it had vanished.[13]

A possible explanation of these incidents is that, unconsciously and via ESP, the people concerned learned that they were in danger, and that they somehow created the apparitional dogs themselves. Alternatively, the phantom dogs may have been created by a higher intelligence acting as a guardian angel.

MYSTERIOUS LIGHT PHENOMENA AND UFOs

After encountering mysterious lights and UFOs, people are sometimes unable to account for periods of time, and they may come to believe that they've experienced temporary abduction by aliens. I'll discuss cases of that type in the next chapter. This chapter will examine a selection of reports concerning mysterious lights and UFOs, where there doesn't appear to be obvious indications of 'missing time' or possible abduction. However, it's conceivable that some of the witnesses mentioned in this chapter *did* experience missing time, but simply didn't notice, or that the investigators who compiled the reports didn't ask their informants about possible missing time, or didn't mention it in their write-ups.

In theory, it's possible to distinguish between anomalous aerial lights and aerial objects that seem to be 'structured craft'. The latter might be more correctly described as UFOs than the former. However, even lights without an identifiable 'structure' sometimes act as if they were under intelligent control. Furthermore, if a witness is unable to discern any structure within or behind aerial lights, it doesn't necessarily mean that there is none. Therefore, I shan't try to draw a hard and fast distinction between 'lights' and 'UFOs'.

Sightings of what are known as 'earth lights' have been reported from numerous places in the UK and elsewhere over the years. (They're known as 'spooklights' or 'ghost lights' in the USA.) They appear in many colours, shapes and sizes. Globular orange forms of basketball size appear to be the most common. Although sporadic, earth lights have been seen recurrently in certain localities, such as the Hessdalen Valley, in Norway, and Longdendale, in England, inviting speculation that they arise from natural forces associated with geological conditions and tectonic strain. However, in some cases, they seem to interact with observers, giving the impression of some sort of controlling intelligence, which is at variance with what one might expect from an impersonal natural phenomenon.

THE LONGDENDALE LIGHTS

Longdendale is a valley that extends from the eastern fringe of the Greater Manchester conurbation into Derbyshire. The busy A628 and a railway line run through the valley, which contains electricity pylons and a series of reservoirs. Bleaklow (633m/2,077ft), the second highest of the Peak District hills, rises to the south of the valley, and the summit of Black Hill (582m/1,909ft) is about 3 miles to the north. Over the years, strange lights have been seen in this area, and many of them may have emanated from points on the land itself. The sightings have sometimes led to mountain rescue personnel being called out.

Paul Devereux states that the lights have been appearing on Bleaklow for hundreds of years, and take different forms. He reports that a powerful beam has been seen in the vicinity of Bramah Edge and Clough Edge (escarpments close to the reservoirs in the floor of the valley), and he also refers to a string of moving and eventually fading lights that often appear in the vicinity of Torside Castle, a mound or hillock about a mile west-north-west of the summit of Bleaklow.[1]

David Clarke[2] and Paul Devereux[3] refer to an unusual experience that befell a woman called Barbara Drabble in Longdendale in July 1970. There are some slight differences between their accounts, but hopefully the following summary, which draws on both versions, is broadly accurate. Mrs Drabble was a trainee teacher and the wife of the local Peak Park Warden. The incident occurred when she was driving home to Crowden. She was travelling along the A628 beside the reservoirs when a brilliant, incandescent, blue light lit up the valley.[4] As she drove into the light she felt intensely cold, and the hairs on the back of her neck stood on end. The strange illumination lasted for several minutes. At the end of her journey, she noticed that the car felt cold and had an icy sheen. When she subsequently asked local farmers about the phenomenon, they seemed uncomfortable and weren't forthcoming. Clarke (pp. 137–138) explains that a year later, people at Crowden Youth Hostel were dazzled by a brilliant light shining through the windows. The local mountain rescue team went on to Bleaklow, since lights had been seen there, but they found nothing.

Close to midnight on 14 February 1995, housewife Laverne Marshall had a frightening experience as she was driving home to Glossop. Her 20-year-old daughter, Stacey, and the latter's baby were in the back seat of the car. The incident began as they were travelling from the top of the Woodhead Pass into Longdendale. Four or five small balls of bright light suddenly appeared on the dashboard of the car and danced up and down. There was no aircraft above, there were no headlights behind the car, and there were no houses around. As Stacey lifted the baby off the back seat and held her, the lights moved to the roof of the car. In her rear-view mirror, Laverne saw them moving around in the car. Stacey activated the central locking and slid the cover over the sunroof. Then, according to Laverne, the lights 'sort of split up into two groups' and went to the rear window before returning, in single file, to the dashboard, where they regrouped. They blinked out when the car reached street lights, the whole episode having lasted 7 minutes.[5]

LIGHT PHENOMENA IN THE MIDLANDS

Jenny Randles describes an incident that occurred one night in August 1988. A couple were driving at night on a road skirting the northern end of Cannock Chase when they saw a circular mass glowing with a deep reddish colour that pulsed. There was a surrounding cloud or mist, which touched the top of a hedge. A semi-solid object seemed to emerge from the cloud or mist. After about half a minute, the pulsing mass disappeared, only to reappear further north a few seconds later. Then it disappeared. While it was present, the witnesses felt a strange sense of calm and sudden quietness. Signs of damage to the hedge were subsequently found. Randles concludes that the phenomenon was probably an atmospheric plasma or an earth light, and she states that the incident occurred in a geologically faulted area.[6]

SIGHTINGS IN THE BONNYBRIDGE AREA OF SCOTLAND

Malcolm Robinson hails from Scotland but moved to England in 1998. He's had a long-standing interest in UFO and paranormal phenomena. In 1979, he set up an investigative group called Strange Phenomena Investigations. In early November 1992, while listening to a local radio station, he heard an item about UFO sightings in the Bonnybridge area of central Scotland. This caught his interest and he subsequently spent much time investigating the area's sightings. On the basis of his involvement in the case, he wrote a lengthy and detailed account of it, titled 'The Bonnybridge UFO Phenomena', which used to be available on the Internet. I've drawn on it for the following three items.

On 27 September 1992, after dropping off his wife in Dunipace, 37-year-old Patrick Forsyth (pseudonym) headed towards his home in Denny along the A872. It was a cool night with scattered cloud. He was driving at about

Bonnybridge, central Scotland.

45mph. Suddenly, he became aware of a strange object some 100 yards ahead. It was circular and two-tiered, with a row of green lights around its bottom rim. It appeared to be hovering 25–40ft above the road. As he got nearer, Forsyth noticed that a car directly in front of him had entered a 'fog bank', which had suddenly appeared from nowhere. Forsyth's two sons were in the back seat of the car, and he called out, 'Boys, can you see this?' They confirmed that they could. Seconds later, their car entered the fog bank and Forsyth became aware of a strange humming sound from above. When the car emerged from the 'fog', the strange object had seemingly disappeared. (Robinson doesn't say how long the car seemed to be in the 'fog'.) Forsyth told Robinson that the fog bank was sharply defined, roughly 10–12ft high, and extended only as far as the white lines in the centre of the road.

The Castlecary railway viaduct crosses the busy A80, not far from Bonnybridge. Robinson's article states that around 8.35 p.m. on 15 January 1993, Ray and Cathy Procek were driving along the A80, approaching the viaduct, when Mrs Procek saw some aerial lights, which she pointed out

The Castlecary railway viaduct, near Bonnybridge.

to her husband. In written testimony, he explained that he soon realised that they belonged to a large craft, because it was silhouetted against a cloud. It was triangular, with its nose pointing west. It was stationary and roughly 300ft above the ground. There were white and pinkish lights on its underside. The couple opened the large sunroof of their vehicle to get a better view. Mrs Procek continued to stare with intense amazement at it. Then, the couple noticed that a similar object was hovering low in the sky a short distance away. Both of the objects were matt black. Mr Procek decided against stopping the car for a better look, and his wife readily accepted that decision. The couple were adamant that the objects weren't conventional flying craft. According to a book by Ron Halliday, they were driving to Cumbernauld, which means that they were heading south at the time of their experience.[7]

In a television programme screened in 1994 (an episode of the series *Strange but True?*), Ray Procek said: 'The back end [of the object] was elliptical, and as we passed underneath it I could see it was triangular in shape and there was a light at each corner.' Ron Halliday's book indicates that the couple opened the sunroof of their car as they passed beneath the viaduct, and it was when they reached the other side that they saw the second UFO, which was identical to the first. Both of the UFOs were completely silent. In the TV programme, Ray Procek explained that the two objects were pointing towards each other.

Malcolm Robinson's article mentioned a story that appeared in the 27 September 1997 issue of *Night and Day*, a colour-supplement magazine of the *Mail on Sunday* newspaper. It concerned a close-proximity UFO sighting in October 1995, experienced by a family who lived near Bonnybridge. Vera Prosser, 51 years old, was driving to a garage near Falkirk, accompanied by her husband and daughter. Noticing a large light in a field, resembling a car's headlight on full beam, they slowed down to about 10mph to get a better look. Suddenly, it began to approach their car, and then was directly over it, with its light shining down through the sunroof. Heather, 13, screamed, 'Get out of here! Get out of here!' Looking up through the sunroof, her mother saw what she described as a thick silvery wire around the bottom of the object. She said that the object was wider than the car and roughly 6ft away from the roof. No sound was heard coming from it, and it suddenly shot away at an incredible rate.

Comments

The UFOs seen by these witnesses may have been actual physical craft. Alternatively, it's possible that they were creations of the moment and perhaps hallucinatory – the products of a resourceful, higher intelligence that has the capacity to confuse and deceive us. At any rate, the Bonnybridge area's days as a UFO hot spot appear to be over – for now, at least.

THE CARRINGTON UFO HOT SPOT

The village of Carrington lies on the western fringe of the Greater Manchester conurbation. Nearby, there's a large industrial site, formerly used by Shell Petrochemicals. Steve Mera and Steve Yarwood relate that in the spring of 1976, five people travelling on a bus from Carrington to Sale saw an object, about the size of a football pitch, hanging motionless over the site. It was rectangular, with large, bright white lights set behind some sort of grid structure. Eventually, it started moving slowly and silently towards Irlam, which is about one and a half miles north-west of the industrial site. Two police officers in Sale (about 3 miles to the east) also saw the object. Later in their article, Mera and Yarwood refer to *nine* witnesses. If that was the case, there must have been two witnesses in addition to the people on the bus and the police officers in Sale.[8]

In their book *Mysteries of the Mersey Valley*, Peter Hough and Jenny Randles also refer to this sighting, but there are some differences in their portrayal. They appear to date the event back to November 1977 rather than the spring of 1976. Along with another investigator, they spoke to one of the witnesses, whom they refer to with the pseudonym June Firswood. She explained that she and three other people, whom she knew by sight, had alighted from a bus and were walking towards Partington (south-west of the industrial site) around 5.45 p.m. when they saw a huge light approach from Carrington Moss and pass over the industrial site in the direction of Irlam. It passed directly over them, without making a sound. As in Mera and Yarwood's version, the object is described as having been rectangular, although not just the length of one football pitch, but the length of *several* of them. There were two white lights behind grills at the front, and a throbbing red light at the back. Firswood reported the matter to the police. A Sergeant Butts confirmed to Hough and Randles that the witness had been genuinely shocked. He contacted the airport (Manchester Airport, presumably) later that evening, but was informed that its radar hadn't tracked anything passing over the industrial site. He compared the sketches drawn by the bus passengers with those drawn by the two policemen in Sale, and it was clear that they depicted the same object. According to Butts, enquiries revealed that there'd been so many lights in the area that suspicions had arisen about illegal helicopter flights, although that hadn't been proven.[9]

Mera and Yarwood's article states that in May 1978, Gerry Mitchell, a former RAF pilot, saw three emerald-green objects moving slowly over the industrial site. Hough and Randles (p. 34) refer to what was presumably the same sighting (since they describe the witness as a former RAF pilot), but they give the year as 1977 and state that he saw three green spheres of light shoot across the sky like comets.

Another incident described by Mera and Yarwood involved a woman (hereafter referred to as 'the informant') who contacted them in the summer of 1994. She and two friends were driving at night near the industrial site when she spotted a small triangular-shaped craft moving slowly across a field to her left. She shouted to the driver to stop, and the three of them got out of the car. As she watched, the informant saw a black object starting to move towards them, about 20ft above the ground. A column of bright blue light dropped to the ground as the object passed over a hedge. But the light didn't diffuse as it went through the hedge – it kept the same shape, as if it were solid. The informant saw the object move silently over the road, into the opposite field. She was distressed to discover that her companions had experienced the incident differently. Although not entirely sure about what had happened, they claimed to have seen a slow-moving aircraft, but in some way it hadn't seemed real.

According to Mera and Yarwood, in February 1996 there were reports of large, triangular UFOs being seen over parts of the Greater Manchester area, such as Bowdon, Carrington and Salford. They refer to UFO sightings in September 2002, including one in which four middle-aged witnesses reportedly saw a huge oblong-shaped craft close to the Carrington industrial site. It had a huge red light at the front, which pulsated about once every 3 seconds. As the UFO approached the area, it was shining a large floodlight. It moved slowly across the sky and disappeared into the distance. The witnesses were amazed that it hadn't been seen and reported by hundreds of other people. Mera and Yarwood explain that there were further UFO sightings in the summer of 2009, although they don't explicitly state that any of them were over the Carrington area.

Comments

Given the discrepancies between Mera and Yarwood's article and Hough and Randles' book with regard to what happened in the 1970s, at least one of these sources must contain historical errors. However, assuming that the accounts are broadly accurate, the witnesses may have experienced paranormal apparitional events of a hallucinatory nature rather than sightings of real aerial objects. If the massive objects allegedly seen over the Carrington area had been real flying craft, we might have expected a large number of other witnesses (perhaps even hundreds or thousands) to come forward, which was apparently not the case. Indeed, the matter might well have become a national news sensation.

SIGHTINGS NEAR WARMINSTER

As noted in Chapter 3, the Warminster area in Wiltshire acquired a reputation for UFO sightings and other oddities in the mid-1960s. According to the late Arthur Shuttlewood, a man called Terry Pell, from Spalding in Lincolnshire, had a dramatic encounter on 10 August 1965 while driving a lorry to Warminster. The incident allegedly occurred early in the morning near Colloway Clump, a hillside copse to the north of the town. Pell's wife and 4-year-old daughter were asleep in the cab beside him. A ball of crimson light shot out of the hillside on his left, flew in an arc, and then hovered 50 yards in front of the lorry before flashing down towards the cab. Pell braked sharply and shielded his eyes as the orb virtually attached itself to the windscreen. However, the lorry's engine had begun to seize as the ball was flying down towards it, and Pell thought that the truck would have stopped anyway. The orb went backwards as the vehicle proceeded forwards before coming to a halt. As the shocked driver sat in his seat, the orb detached itself and went into the sky. Pell told Shuttlewood that it was 'a good thirty to forty feet across at the base', which is a curious description if Shuttlewood is correct in referring to it as a 'spheroid'. Pell reportedly said that the object resembled a human eye as it came close, and that when it was fixed to the windscreen, its metallic edges produced enormous vibration, although the glass didn't break. When his eyes had recovered from the glare, he saw the object hovering over Colloway Clump for a few seconds. It then vanished, only to be seen again, gleaming pale gold and then yellow, just above the trees on the horizon.[10]

In their critical appraisal of the Warminster case, Steve Dewey and John Ries refer to what appears to be a different version of this story.[11] It appeared in a book by Brad Steiger, who gives the driver's surname as Simpson, not Pell, and gives a different time for the event (5.25 a.m. rather than 4.36 a.m.).[12] Steiger's version is less dramatic than Shuttlewood's. According to Dewey and Ries, Steiger got the report through a US-based news agency. Dewey and Ries assume that Shuttlewood 'originally wrote [it] for media or wire services'. Therefore, it may be that when Shuttlewood came to include the story in *The Warminster Mystery*, he embellished it.

According to Shuttlewood's second book, *Warnings from Flying Friends*, a Dennis Tilt and his wife had a memorable experience as they were driving home to Warminster on the night of 22 October 1966. In the vicinity of Chitterne – a village about 6 miles to the east of Warminster, as the crow flies – they saw three flame-coloured lights in a triangular formation on farmland to their right. Mr Tilt stopped the car and got out to view the spectacle. But his wife felt a little apprehensive, so he got back in and drove off. Then, looking back, the couple noticed that the lights had fused together. The object was now in the sky and huge. Resembling a frying pan without a handle, it was silverish and was hovering about 50ft above the ground. The Tilts sped away. The UFO gave off a fitful yellow glow and seemed to maintain a steady distance from the car, although it had seemingly gone by the time the couple reached the street where they lived (St John's Road). But when Mrs Tilt was straightening some curtains, she saw it again for a few seconds. Before blacking out, it suddenly changed to an elongated egg shape. Mr Tilt called at the farm concerned in the morning, but the farmer was unable to enlighten him. Mr Tilt didn't know the precise spot from which the UFO had taken off, and he couldn't discern any telltale marks or indentations in the relevant area. He checked with the Army, but received answers convincing him that the sighting wasn't connected with them.[13]

Comments

As noted, the three flame-coloured lights allegedly seen by the Tilts fused into one huge 'object', and Mrs Tilt eventually saw it take an elongated egg-like shape. Shape-shifting has been noted in other reports of UFO sightings, and to my mind poses a challenge to the notion that these 'objects' are spacecraft. I think it makes more sense to construe such events as orchestrated theatrical displays.

UFO PHENOMENA IN SOUTH-WEST WALES

By the second half of the 1970s, reports of anomalous phenomena in the Warminster area seemed to be on the wane. In 1977, south-west Wales appeared to become a new hot spot. The alleged incidents occurred mainly in Pembrokeshire and were largely confined to that year. However, there are conflicting stories about many of the events, with indications that some of the accounts were invented or grossly exaggerated. I've provided a fairly detailed overview of the matter in Chapter 8 of my book *Zones of Strangeness*.

Stephen Taylor's experiences

Seventeen-year-old Stephen Taylor reportedly had some unusual experiences on the evening of 13 March 1977 while walking home from his girlfriend's residence. He related them to Randall Pugh, a UFO researcher and co-author of *The Dyfed Enigma*, a book about the south-west Wales phenomena.[14] At a place called Hendre Bridge, Taylor saw a glowing, oval object in the sky. It had an orange halo. He made a detour to call on some friends, to tell them about the sighting. On his way there, he saw a large black dog racing away from the area where he'd seen the object. His friends laughed at him about the aerial sighting. Continuing his walk home, he got to a point where he should have been able to see the lights of the airbase at RAF Brawdy, but he couldn't. He went over to a gate and leaned on it, to light a cigarette. The lights of the base were obscured by a very large object sitting in a field. He gazed at it for a few minutes before hearing a movement. When he looked, he saw a figure, about 6ft tall, with very high cheek bones and wearing some sort of suit. There was something in the entity's mouth, resembling the breathing apparatus used by divers. Taylor didn't notice any hair, but the entity's eyes were large. In Taylor's words, he 'took a swing' at the figure, but he didn't feel any contact. He then turned and ran. When he got home, his dog acted uncharacteristically, by barking and growling at him.

A STRANGE EXPERIENCE ON DARTMOOR

A cyclist called Maurice Dart had a strange experience on Dartmoor one sunny morning in the summer of 1955. He related it to Michael Williams, the author of a booklet titled *Supernatural Dartmoor*. Having cycled through Postbridge, Dart was heading in the direction of Princetown, along a stretch of road bounded by woodland, when a feeling of panic gripped him. Looking back over his left shoulder, he saw what appeared to be a swirling cloudy mass rapidly descending towards him from the otherwise clear blue sky. He changed down a gear and pedalled hard and fast. He passed through Two Bridges and was cycling uphill when the feeling of panic left him as suddenly as it had come. Looking over his shoulder again, he glimpsed the fuzzy mass disappearing up into the sky, way behind him.[15]

UFO EXPERIENCES INVOLVING 'MISSING TIME'

The notion of alien abduction is controversial. Some people believe that aliens exist and that they really do physically abduct humans. At the other extreme, there are those who regard the supposed aliens as pure fiction, and the memories of the alleged abductees as fantasies or delusions. If abductions are physically real events, where are the abductees taken? Is it to somewhere within the space and time that we occupy, or to a different type of space and time, in a parallel reality?

Another possibility is that an external intelligence is able to manipulate human consciousness, creating an illusion that a physical abduction has occurred. If so, the abduction scenario might entail induced hallucinations and/or implanted false memories. Physical effects might also be orchestrated, to reinforce the impression that a physical abduction has occurred. For example, marks might be produced on a person's body, making it seem that he or she has undergone some sort of medical procedure.

Suffice it to say that I don't pretend to have hard and fast answers. But for ease of expression in what follows, I'll refrain from repeatedly using 'distancing terminology' ('alleged', 'purported', 'ostensible', etc.). For example, if a woman reports memories of abduction, I'll refer to her as an abductee rather than as an alleged abductee. However, I don't mean to imply that memories of alien abduction are necessarily based on real, physical abductions.

Witnessing bizarre and unexpected paranormal phenomena can be frightening, and experiencing abduction by other-worldly beings, or believing that one has been abducted, can be nightmarish. Having a one-off traumatic experience is bad enough, but alien abduction experiences can be recurrent. Abductees can find themselves living in fear, dreading the 'next visit'. However, it's worth noting that a minority of abductees believe that their experiences have in some sense been uplifting or positive. That was so in one of the cases reported below (concerning a family's experience near High Bentham in North Yorkshire). A positive reaction is probably more likely if people construe their abductors as benevolent beings with their best interests at heart.

A FRIGHTENING ENCOUNTER IN GLASGOW

Susan (pseudonym) is in her 60s. She and a friend had a disturbing UFO experience in Glasgow when they were about 13. The incident occurred one night when they were heading home from a café where they worked part-time. They alighted from a bus around 10.45 p.m. and saw a light in the sky, which Susan assumed was a plane. They set off down a quiet lane. A woman was walking ahead of them.

The source of the light seemed to be motionless, but then it moved, very quickly, to another position. It seemed to remain stationary for a few seconds and then it moved again, at very high speed, to another position, each of these movements bringing it closer. By then, Susan had realised that it wasn't an ordinary aircraft. She was able to make out some features. It seemed to be a large, black or dark-grey circular object, with a protuberance on top. Susan wasn't sure whether the protuberance itself was round. There were two flashing red lights opposite each other on the underside of the circular base. And there was a circle of other lights (not coloured) on the underside, close to the edge. They may have been shimmering.

The UFO made further movements, bringing it closer to Susan and her companion. They stopped and stared, and were unable to move. The woman ahead of them was closer to the UFO. She screamed, 'Oh, my God!' and ran back. She took hold of the girls, and the three of them ran towards, and huddled against, a locked gate. The woman made the sign of the cross and the girls did likewise. The woman said, 'Hold together!' Then, they were strongly illuminated from above. After what Susan took to be 3 minutes at the most, things went dark again. When she looked, she saw that the UFO was still quite close, perhaps 100 yards or so away. The woman and the girls resumed their journey. After one or two further movements, the UFO took up a position in the sky in front of them, but somewhat to their right. Shortly after (perhaps within a few minutes), it shot up into the sky and disappeared.

Susan arrived home some 50 minutes later than she would have expected, and she informed me that her friend also experienced missing time. But Susan has since lost touch with her. Therefore, I was unable to obtain testimony from the friend.

THE A70 ENCOUNTER

Gary Wood and Colin Wright had an unusual experience one night in August 1992. UFO researcher Malcolm Robinson was subsequently in touch with them, and has written about the case.[1] The author and researcher Ron Halliday managed to interview at least one of the men, and has also written about it.[2] His portrayal differs in some details from Robinson's. I ran into Gary Wood at a conference in Edinburgh in 2015. I asked him whether I could e-mail some queries to him, given the discrepancies between the versions I've just mentioned. He said that would be all right, but he didn't, in fact, respond to my e-mail enquiries. In retrospect, I wish that I'd conducted a short interview with him at the time of our meeting.

Wood and Wright were driving on the A70, in a rural area south-west of Edinburgh, when their experience began. In the vicinity of Harperrig Reservoir (West Lothian), they saw a two-tiered, disc-shaped object hovering over the road. (Halliday states that Wood and Wright saw the UFO as they were driving towards the reservoir, whereas Robinson states that they had just passed it.) Wood, who was doing the driving, put his foot down on the accelerator, hoping to get away from the UFO by driving under it. As their vehicle approached it, the UFO appeared to emit some sort of shimmering mist, which touched the car, whereupon Wood and Wright were temporarily enveloped in a black void for what seemed like seconds. The car shuddered and they regained their sight.

Wood had to fight to regain control of the car, since it was now on the wrong side of the road. When the men arrived in the village of Tarbrax, where they were due to drop off a satellite TV system, they discovered

The A70 road at Harperrig Reservoir.

that they were much later than expected. According to Halliday, they'd begun their journey around 10 p.m. and had arrived at Tarbrax at 12.45 the next morning. But Robinson states that they set out from Edinburgh just after 11.30 p.m. He indicates that the journey should have taken about ½ an hour, but the men were told that they were about 1½ hours late. (However, two sentences later, he refers to the journey itself as having taken 1½ hours.) They subsequently underwent hypnosis sessions, and each of them recalled an alien abduction scenario and being subjected to a medical-type examination, although there were some differences between their recollections. Robinson (p. 39) notes that the men came back from their encounter with physical marks that weren't there previously: Wright had a strange scar at the base of his penis, and Wood had a strange mark on the back of his neck. However, I suppose it's possible that those marks were present before the event in question and had simply gone unnoticed.

Comments

The use of hypnosis to elicit recollections of supposed abduction experiences is controversial, given the possibility of fantasy and suggestion creating false memories. However, setting aside the hypnotically elicited material, the A70 case is still intriguing. In terms of an environmental theory, it might be suggested that the two men had experienced an electromagnetic event that had affected their brains, causing a period of amnesia. However, it's noteworthy that Wood's amnesia appears to have begun and ended at the same time as Wright's. Given that people's physiology varies, that would perhaps be surprising if they were responding to some sort of ambient magnetic field or radiation. Also, there's the question of where they and their car were during the period of missing time. Are we to suppose that they pulled off the road and sat in the vehicle in some sort of trance state for a lengthy period, and that while still in that state, Wood was able to drive away before he and his companion snapped back into normal consciousness? On the other hand, if the event is construed as an actual physical abduction, there's still the question of what happened to the car during that period.

In her book *Time Storms*, Jenny Randles discusses cases in which people have experienced mysterious spatial and temporal displacements after encountering strange clouds or mists, and she refers to the A70 case.[3] She calls these events *time storms* – hence the title of her book – and she views them as phenomena, of an electromagnetic nature, that have the capacity to affect both space and time. Imagine, for example, that a couple in a car encounter a strange mist and then find themselves, unexpectedly, miles from where they thought they were, and that it is 3 hours later than they thought. From Randles' perspective, if I've understood it correctly, this could mean that they had, in effect, been teleported to the new location and had literally travelled through time to the near future. If so, there would be no 'missing time' (a period that they'd lived through but couldn't remember). Applying this notion to the A70 case, it might be conjectured that Gary Wood and Colin Wright jumped ahead in time and didn't actually live through the period that they couldn't recall.

Jenny Randles seems to view time storms as impersonal phenomena rather than manifestations of a directing intelligence. Therefore, in using the word 'teleported' in the previous paragraph, I don't mean to imply that she is suggesting that anyone or anything deliberately brings about the effects.

She contends that these phenomena can be misunderstood as UFO-related events, involving abduction, particularly if investigators employ hypnosis to try to help the witnesses recall what happened during the supposed period of missing time, as happened in the case of Wood and Wright. In Randles' view, hypnotically elicited memories can be very inaccurate, and can be shaped by expectations and cultural beliefs. However, I have some misgivings about Randles' interpretation of 'time storm' phenomena, and I'll return to this topic in the next chapter.

MISSING TIME IN ARMADALE

Ron Halliday describes an interesting case from Armadale, West Lothian, involving a man whom he refers to as Andrew Swan. During the evening of 30 July 1994 there was an electrical storm, and Swan drove to a vantage point, a few minutes away, near a local secondary school, to observe the lightning. He parked his Audi and caught sight of a large, pyramid-shaped UFO behind a row of trees, a few hundred yards away. He noted that his watch gave the time as 11.45 p.m. He decided to drive to another viewpoint, on the other side of the hovering object. The UFO that he'd been watching, or a second one, flew down low, very close to the roof of his car. The UFO suddenly halted, and Swan made an emergency stop. Standing at the side of the road, he could clearly make out an inverted pyramid shape, floating just above, or in front of, an industrial waste tip. He tried to illuminate the UFO with a halogen spotlight, but the bulb exploded as soon as the beam hit the UFO. He decided to leave, but the engine of his car failed to start when he turned the ignition key. He'd already called the police, and he was frustrated by their delay in arriving. He eventually made a further effort to start the car, but in vain. The UFO shot into the air and flew over him at high speed. He made a second call to the police, but a patrol car was on its way and soon arrived. The AA was called. The mechanic was unable to start Swan's car, so it was towed away. However, it was subsequently found to be in working order. Another mystery concerned the timing of these events: the police computer had logged Swan's first call at 2 a.m., although he believed that he'd made it before midnight. It appeared that a lot more time had passed than Swan could account for.[4]

CASES FROM NORTH YORKSHIRE

An encounter on the A65

I'm aware of three sources for this next case. They differ regarding some of the details. I've drawn mainly on the version given in a book by Carl Nagaitis and Philip Mantle.[5] Hopefully what follows is a reasonably accurate portrayal of what happened. Nagaitis and Mantle refer to the witness, pseudonymously, as Christine Smith. She was 36 at the time.

It was 4 March 1982, and Smith was driving home to Skipton after visiting her mother in Morecambe, Lancashire. The unusual events began around 10.15 p.m. (or about 10.30 p.m., according to Paul Devereux[6]). Nagaitis and Mantle mention Coniston Cutting on the A65, but they don't explicitly state that Smith had reached it by the time her unusual experience began. However, I understand from Philip Mantle (e-mail, January 2012) that she had.

Coniston Cutting on the A65.

Smith noticed that the right side of her car seemed to be illuminated with a soft, bluish light. Then, in her right-side wing mirror, she saw two strange lights, behind and just above the height of her vehicle. They were about the size of car headlamps. One was royal blue. The other was a vivid red. They seemed to be following her car and, at times, she thought she could see smaller lights behind them. However, when she looked in her rear-view mirror, she saw only blackness. Her family's sheepdog was with her in the car, but was asleep. As she drove out of the cutting, a beam of pure white light shot down from above, illuminating the road on her nearside. A circle of light fell on to the fields and then moved on to the road, and suddenly the car was encircled. (It's not clear from Nagaitis and Mantle's account whether this circle of light was from the beam that had lit up the road on Smith's nearside, but I presume that's what they mean.) Although the heater was on, Smith suddenly felt very cold, and the engine of the car seemed to be revving much more than it should have been. Eventually, the headlamps of an oncoming heavy vehicle appeared on the horizon, whereupon the beam from above flicked out and the pursuing red and blue lights vanished. But Smith's feeling of terror persisted for a while, since she wondered whether they would return. However, according to a book by the late Tony Dodd, she *didn't* feel afraid or panicky during the journey.[7]

When she got home Smith felt greatly relieved, but physically and mentally drained, and she felt completely exhausted for a further week. Although she hadn't been held up by traffic, her journey had taken 95 minutes instead of the usual hour. (But according to Dodd, she reported that she was *an hour late* in arriving home.) And the next day, she discovered that she had a rash on her back and chest. She eventually underwent three hypnosis sessions, in the course of which she mentioned contact with aliens who had supposedly been visiting Earth for centuries. During one of the sessions, an entity calling itself Zeus supposedly spoke through her. But, as already noted, there's controversy about the use of hypnosis in UFO research, and some might argue that 'Zeus' was really Smith herself, putting on a theatrical performance, albeit perhaps unconsciously. Similar considerations arise in relation to claims that discarnate spirits can communicate with the living through spiritualist mediums, although some researchers believe that mediums can provide cogent evidence for survival after death (see, for example, *Is There an Afterlife?*, a book by the late David Fontana).

As noted, Smith reportedly heard her car's engine revving loudly. At the time, there was a light coming down from above. Was the car's clutch slipping, or was Smith's perception being affected by some sort of energy field? Alternatively, was a UFO exercising an antigravity effect on the car, making the wheels lose contact with the road surface or have less traction? If so, was the car also being propelled forward by a mysterious force?

Incident near High Bentham

The small town of High Bentham is located about 2½ miles south-south-west of Ingleton, North Yorkshire. To the south of High Bentham, across the Lancashire border, there's an area of hilly moorland, known as the Forest of Bowland. The High Bentham area was the setting for a UFO sighting on the evening of Sunday, 16 January 2005. The witnesses were Ann (then aged 58), her daughter Rachel (then aged 35) and Rachel's two sons, Alex and Benjamin (then aged 11 and 9, respectively). I'll refer to them, collectively, as 'the family'. The next day, Ann notified a local radio station of their sighting, and it appeared that at least four other people – two in Clitheroe, one in Feniscowles and one in Leyland – had also seen a UFO the previous day. Ann informs me that these sightings occurred after 6.30 p.m. Obviously, though, it's impossible to know for sure whether everyone saw the same UFO.

Ann also reported the family's sighting to Joe McGonagle, a Staffordshire-based UFO researcher. He referred the matter to the Lancashire Anomalous Phenomena Investigation Society (LAPIS), which investigated the case. But along with a companion, McGonagle also visited the family at their then home, a couple of miles south of High Bentham, over the county boundary, in north Lancashire.

For this summary, I've drawn on several sources: (1) Information from Ann and another member of the family; (2) Information from Joe McGonagle; (3) A television programme, recorded in 2005, featuring the case;[8] (4) An Internet article by Sam Willey.[9] He gives his source as the 'LAPIS UFO Group', although I gather that he wasn't personally involved in the LAPIS investigation.

The family had a meal at a Little Chef restaurant (now closed) on the A65, and then set off for home. (In the TV programme, Rachel explained that they left the restaurant between about 5.20 and 5.30 p.m., and Ann stated that the journey should have taken about 20 minutes.) With Rachel driving, they headed up the A65 to Ingleton, a distance of approximately 3 miles, and turned left into Tatterthorn Lane. The lane goes south-west for about a third of a mile and then bends sharply to the left. At the bend, there's

Tatterthorn Lane, near High Bentham.

a row of terraced houses projecting out to the right. In the car, there was some mention of how the chimneys were silhouetted against the sky. But it's unclear precisely what happened during the next stage of their journey, before the family found themselves driving into High Bentham. (During a visit to the area at the end of January 2012, I retraced the route from the site of the former restaurant to High Bentham. I was accompanied by Ann.)

In the TV programme, Rachel said that the next thing she remembered, after the chimneys were mentioned, was 'seeing this awesome bright light'. Ann reported that she saw a light rising up and then hovering above the car. And according to one of the boys, it hovered for a while and then shot off. Sam Willey's article states that after it hovered over the car, the object accelerated downwards at an amazing speed, and then gained altitude and sped away over the hills of the Forest of Bowland. However, in the TV programme, no one from the family said that the object had accelerated downwards and then regained altitude, and neither Ann nor my other contact in the family indicated that it had done that.

Ann told me that when they arrived home, it was 6.50 p.m. and they felt as if they'd 'missed something' (i.e. that they didn't have full recall). But I gather that three of them, if not all four, subsequently had recollections suggestive of contact with some form of intelligence. However, it wasn't until 10 days later (after three of them tried to retrace their route) that it actually dawned on them that they'd arrived home significantly late on the evening in question. I raised with Ann the possibility that they'd simply made a mistake, and had arrived home at 5.50 p.m., not 6.50 p.m. However, she insisted that it was the latter, and she said that she recalled turning on the television to watch the 7 o'clock news. My other contact in the family informed me that their period of missing time had covered the period 5.40 p.m. to 6.40 p.m., which is broadly consistent with Ann's recollection of when they got home. (The mysterious part of their journey – the phase during which they saw the UFO and had only partial recall – had apparently ended by the time they found themselves driving into High Bentham. But at that point, they still had a couple of miles or so to go before reaching their home.)

The TV programme showed the family members describing their positive emotional reaction to the UFO. For example, Rachel commented: '[We] all felt that it was like just this absolutely overwhelming love that you just felt from it,' and Ann said that they felt a sense of loss when it had gone. Rachel also described how things returned to normal: 'Then it was like' – snapping her fingers – 'all of a sudden, and then I was driving, and the noise was back.' Presumably, then, up to that point, they'd experienced a period of silence, or relative silence, which is a fairly common accompaniment of paranormal experiences.

As noted, three members of the family tried to retrace the route they'd taken. In respect of the original incident, they recalled that at one stage they'd been on a straight, wide road that was high up. But instead, they found only a country lane. They tried a different route, but it, too, seemed wrong. Around that time, they experienced a tingling sensation. It eased off to some degree, but then increased again when they turned round and drove back along the part of the road where they'd first experienced it. At that point, the engine of the car cut out! Two of them got a lift home. Rachel, who had been doing the driving, managed to restart the car and get it to a garage. She was told that the coil had burnt out.

In the fourth paragraph of his article, Sam Willey states that LAPIS thought that the family had experienced 20 minutes of missing time, although he goes on to say (in his sixth paragraph) that it eventually became clear that they'd experienced over an hour of missing time. Certainly, if we assume that they left the restaurant between 5.20 and 5.30 p.m. on the day in question (16 January 2005) and didn't get home until 6.50 p.m., a substantial amount of time is unaccounted for.

Willey indicates that LAPIS kept in touch with the family and learned of other developments. For example, he states that there were problems with electrical items in their home, and that Ann recalled that she'd seen a strange triangular-shaped craft when she was a child. Ann informed me that the family had indeed experienced a good many strange things over the years. For instance, she explained that on 26 January 2005, the day when three of them tried to retrace their route home from the restaurant, the unusual events went beyond the tingling sensation and the car breakdown. But she said that for the time being, at least, they didn't want to publicise further information about their unusual experiences.

In connection with the TV documentary, Rachel underwent hypnotic regression. A snippet of the regression session was included in the TV programme, but it was too brief to be very informative. However, according to Sam Willey's article, Rachel mentioned the 'missing road' that LAPIS had been trying to find, describing it as a stretch of road in the air.

It's hard to know what really happened when the family drove home on the evening of 16 January 2005. Did they experience a collective vision of being on a straight, wide and elevated road? Or did an external intelligence edit their memories? If so, their recollection of being on a wide, straight road may have been a paranormally imposed false memory. That could also explain Rachel's recollection, under hypnosis, of a road in the air. It's also conceivable that their recollection of when they arrived home was a deliberately instilled pseudo-memory. If so, there may have been *no* missing time, or less of it than they thought, even though their overall experience would still have been decidedly paranormal. But, as noted above, Ann is convinced that they *did* arrive home late. Of course, it would help if there were independent evidence of when they left the restaurant and got home. Joe McGonagle informed me that their restaurant bill was paid with a credit card, and that he asked whether they had a copy of the payment slip, which would have been time-stamped. But he was told that they'd lost it. Ann informed me that subsequent to the incident of 16 January 2005, they were provided with a copy of the receipt or credit card slip by someone at the restaurant, although that item of potentially corroborative evidence was also lost or discarded.

This could be construed as a classic case of the alien abduction type, with different generations of the same family being involved. It's certainly an interesting case, given that there were four witnesses to the events of 16 January 2005 (or eight, if we include the people in Lancashire who reportedly saw what may have been the same UFO).

In many abduction cases, the participants find the events traumatic, but with this family, positive emotions have been reported as well as perplexity and fear. It's also worth noting that the manifestations in this case included physical effects. For example, when three members of the family were having strange tingling sensations, their car broke down, although it's conceivable that that was purely coincidental.

Of course, cases of this type raise intriguing questions. For example, if a driver experiences missing time, what happens to his or her vehicle during that period? Did Rachel park the car somewhere and sit in it, entranced, along with her mother and sons, for an hour or more? Or were they and the car temporarily spirited away to another place?

ALAN GODFREY'S EXPERIENCE IN TODMORDEN, WEST YORKSHIRE

One of the best-known reports concerning an encounter with a structured craft and subsequent missing time comes from 1980, and concerns Alan Godfrey, who was then a 33-year-old police constable. Not long after the incident, Jenny Randles wrote about it in her book *The Pennine UFO Mystery*.[10] Godfrey himself described his experience in the third episode of a four-part Channel 5 television series called *Britain's Closest Encounters*.[11] The programme was broadcast in July 2008. There are some discrepancies between Godfrey's testimony in the television programme and the account in Randles' book, but they are relatively minor. The following summary draws on both sources.

The encounter began shortly after 5 a.m. on 29 November 1980. Godfrey was driving a police car on Burnley Road in Todmorden, West Yorkshire. He was investigating a report of some cows having been seen wandering through a housing estate. He encountered a dome-shaped object that was hovering 5ft above the road. He stopped the car within 100ft of it (according to Randles' book), or within about 20 yards of it (according to what he said in the Channel 5 television programme). It was the size of a bus seen sideways on, and had what looked like a row of windows. Things were eerily silent. The bottom section of the object seemed to be rotating, and the bushes and trees by the roadside were shaking. Godfrey tried to call for assistance, but neither his car radio nor his personal radio worked. He sat in his vehicle and sketched the object in front of him. His next recollection was of finding himself further along the road, driving the car. He stopped, got out and observed that the object had gone. According to Randles' book, he drove to the town centre, picked up a colleague, and returned with him to the scene. There were blotchy dry patches on the part of the road over which the UFO had hovered, but elsewhere the road was wet with rain. The book relates that the officers then drove back to the police station and that Godfrey noticed that it was 5.30 a.m. The book implies that this was later than he would have thought. But according to the Channel 5 programme, after noticing that the UFO had gone, Godfrey drove straight back to the police station – the programme made no mention of his picking up a colleague and returning to the scene. If what Godfrey reported in the television programme was correct, it must have been later than 5.30 a.m. when he got back to the station, because he said that he'd been away for around 45–50 minutes (although he was unable to account for about 30–35 minutes of that period).

After the incident, there was an itchy patch on the instep of Godfrey's left foot, and the sole of his left police boot bore a distinct transverse crack. Randles (p. 128) notes that a motorist reported having seen a bluish-white object meandering along a valley at Cliviger (Lancashire), a few miles north-west of Todmorden, around 5 a.m. that same morning. She also mentions (p. 129) a caretaker who worked at a school overlooking the site of Godfrey's encounter. About 12 hours after Godfrey's experience, the caretaker reportedly saw a bright light that moved along the valley below and then shot into the sky. In addition, Randles (pp. 128–129) refers to UFO sightings, not far from Todmorden, reported by three police officers from the Halifax force. They had supposedly occurred around the time of Godfrey's experience. However, a magazine article by Peter Brookesmith, David Clarke and Andy Roberts cites evidence indicating that the three officers had had their sightings several days previously.[12]

Members of the Manchester UFO Research Association took an interest in the Godfrey case, and he agreed to undergo some hypnosis sessions. There were four in all, which occurred during the late summer and early autumn of 1981. Unfortunately, I don't find the description of them given by Randles entirely clear. Therefore, I shan't attempt to summarise her account of them. Suffice it to say that Godfrey's recollections could be seen as indicating an alien entity encounter or some sort of visionary experience with religious overtones, although another possibility is that the hypnotically elicited material was the product of fantasy rather than true recall, or an amalgam of real memories and imagination.

According to a book by Paul Weatherhead, Godfrey admitted to having read some books on UFOs in the period between his encounter and the hypnotic regression sessions.[13] Possibly, then, his recollections were influenced by what he'd read. Weatherhead (pp. 50–51) also mentions some other unusual experiences that had befallen Godfrey. For example, in 1965, while driving a van, he suddenly braked, believing that he'd just hit a woman with a dog who had stepped out on to the road. But when he got out of the vehicle, he found no trace of the woman or dog, and he discovered that it was 2 hours later than he thought. In their magazine article, Brookesmith, Clarke and Roberts quote from a personal communication to them from Jenny Randles. It stated that Godfrey was with a girlfriend at the time of the incident in the van, and it seemed to imply that *both of them* had experienced missing time.

Weatherhead (p. 47 and p. 50) refers to speculation that Godfrey suffered from narcolepsy, a disorder that can result in hallucinations. In a similar vein, UFO sceptic Andy Roberts, appearing in the aforementioned Channel 5 television programme, opined that Godfrey had gone into 'some form of altered state of consciousness' and may have misperceived a bus. This notion is also discussed in the article by Brookesmith, Clarke and Roberts, which tries to account for Godfrey's experience in prosaic terms. For my part, though, I don't think we should dismiss the possibility that he had a genuinely paranormal experience.

AN INTERRUPTED JOURNEY ON THE A646

Nagaitis and Mantle's book describes some strange experiences that a lorry driver had on 14 January 1980 (pp. 155–158). William Barrett, 55 years old, set off from his home in Burnley, Lancashire, well before 6 a.m. He had to drop off a package in Todmorden and then proceed to Hollingworth, near Oldham, to pick up a load. He drove towards Todmorden on the A646. About halfway there, he heard a noise similar to that of an electricity generator. Then, within seconds, his headlights illuminated an odd shape in a lay-by ahead: a stationary, dark, metallic object resting on the ground, with three red rays projecting down from it to the ground. There appeared to be two people moving about. He assumed they were workmen. When he got nearer, the beams seemed less red. There was a curved pipe on top of the object, and he wondered whether he was seeing a secret weapon. Slowing down to a crawl, he noticed that one of the figures had a peaked cap and a dark, two-piece uniform, while the other seemed to be clad in a one-piece grey or silver suit and was stooping down, with bent knees, to look at the object.

As he drew away from the lay-by, Barrett continued to look at the scene, hoping to get some further clue about what was going on. Suddenly, his headlights failed and he was plunged into darkness. He jammed on his brakes. As the truck came to a halt, he blacked out. He was brought back to consciousness by a sudden jolting sensation, and he found that the engine of the lorry was running and the lights were working again. But, as he later realised, he was a quarter of a mile further along the road.

Barrett dropped off the parcel in Todmorden and then continued his journey. When he reached his destination, he was told that it was 9.10 a.m. The journey, which should have taken 1¼ hours, had taken 3 hours and 25 minutes! Driving home, he was troubled by pain in his left leg. There was a bruise just behind and above his left knee, although he didn't know how he'd acquired it. Feeling very tired, he went to bed and tried to forget about the incident.

Nearly 2 years later, Barrett read about Alan Godfrey's experience in a national newspaper. The report included a photograph of Godfrey with Mons Mill, a Todmorden landmark, in the background. Barrett had passed the mill after regaining consciousness following his own encounter. In 1984, Barrett's experience came to the attention of the British UFO Research Association. He apparently believed that he'd witnessed the abduction of Alan Godfrey, although that would have been impossible by normal criteria, given that Godfrey's experience had occurred some distance from the site of Barrett's, and had happened about 10 months later.

THE DARESBURY AREA, CHESHIRE

Peter Hough and Jenny Randles refer to a small area of north Cheshire that includes the village of Daresbury, which was the birthplace of Charles Dodgson, better known as Lewis Carroll.[14] His writings included *Alice's Adventures in Wonderland*. Drawing on this literary connection, Hough and

Randles give the area the whimsical name 'Wonderland'. They contend that it's probably the 'centre point of high weirdness' in England, 'where anything can happen and usually does'. However, they don't define its boundaries precisely. They state that its essence is a small triangle of land located, roughly, between Helsby Hill, the town of Runcorn and the villages of Daresbury and Moore.

Missing time at a building site

Hough and Randles (p. 94) mention a story that they obtained from a security firm, although they don't specify whether they actually spoke to the witnesses. And they're vague about the location. However, in a magazine article, Randles states that the incident occurred 'on the banks of the Mersey, at Moore, Cheshire', in 1977.[15] An experienced security guard and a trainee were protecting a building site. Just after they'd made a scheduled call to their base at 1 a.m., a blinding light filled the small wooden hut they were in. In terror, they hid under a table, although one of them felt that there was something beautiful and hypnotic about the light. A humming noise filled the yard outside. They were found, still under the table, by another security guard, who was sent to check on them after they'd failed to make a scheduled call to their base at 2 a.m. They reportedly thought that only 20 minutes had passed. A white misty powder, resembling dry ice ('seemingly ice crystals', according to Randles' magazine article) was found at the spot where they said that an object had landed.

A motorcyclist's experience

A motorcyclist called Billy Lowry reportedly experienced some unusual events on the night of 1 September 1983.[16] He was travelling north on the A49, in the direction of Warrington. He recalled seeing a strange light in the sky and stopping to look at it. He was apparently on a quiet stretch of road between Weaverham and Acton Bridge. He dismounted from his machine, switched off the lights, and stood in the middle of the road, looking at the sky. Although he was on a bend in the road and putting himself at risk of being struck by another vehicle, he felt compelled to do so. He saw a dark, wedge-shaped mass above him. There were several lights on the object, which was moving very slowly and silently. A car appeared around the bend. Its driver wound down his window, slowed to a crawl and drove around Lowry without stopping. Lowry thought about photographing the object, but a mental voice told him not to. He rode away, but then saw a sign indicating that he was 4 miles from Chester, which wasn't on his route. He was on the wrong road, the A56, and heading in the wrong direction – south-west. He stopped to reorient himself, and checked the time. It was now 2.15 a.m. He was unable to account for a period of over 1½ hours.

AN ENCOUNTER NEAR WARMINSTER

This case was drawn to my attention by Steve Wills, a Warminster-based UFO researcher, and I've since been in touch with the witness herself, Amanda Holbrook. She reports an incident that occurred on the B3095 in 1970 or 1971, when she was 10 years old. At the time, she and her family were living in Monkton Deverill, a village about 4½ miles south of Warminster.

Amanda and her parents had been out for the evening in West Ashton, near Trowbridge, and were heading home. She was in the back seat of the family car. As they came out of Brixton Deverill (less than a mile from their home) and passed some trees, the car came to a sudden stop and started vibrating. Amanda recalls that it was illuminated by an intense light. She was aware of something beside her and at first felt scared. Then, it seemed as if some sort of dark wall had been put up, which made her feel very calm. She recalls that she 'talked and talked', although she can't remember what she was speaking about. The bright light moved away, and Amanda noticed that her parents were shaking. The engine of the car was now running normally. When they got home, Amanda's sister came downstairs in her dressing gown and asked why they were so late. As Amanda puts it, 'We had lost an hour of time.' Her mother advised her not to mention the incident to other people, since they would think that she was mad. Referring to the incident later in her life, her mother said that she recalled seeing a triangular-shaped object flying away.

Amanda's parents are now both dead. Shortly after the incident, her mother started being troubled by large blisters, all over her body, and the problem persisted for years, although doctors didn't have an explanation for them. Amanda's father refused to discuss the incident, although – as she put it to me – 'that was how he was'. However, he became quite withdrawn and depressed soon after the encounter, and remained that way for the next few years. Amanda herself was diagnosed with multiple sclerosis when she was 42, although it's thought that the disease had been present for many years prior to that. She has to use a wheelchair, but she seems to have a positive attitude to life.

Amanda told me that her mother's side of the family was of Romany descent, and that she (Amanda) and other family members have had psychic experiences. For example, she recalled a time (possibly when she was in her 20s) when she had a feeling that a friend, John, shouldn't use his motorbike. She told him so. Within 2 days, he and a pillion passenger were fatally injured in an accident. Amanda has a son and a daughter, aged 37 and 33 respectively at the time of my speaking to her (March 2017). When her son was about 4 or 5, he had 'little friends' (Amanda's words). Were these imaginary friends, or was he experiencing something paranormal? Her daughter has a history of sleepwalking and never sleeps without a light on. She had apparitional experiences when she was a child.

Comments

It's noteworthy that the incident on the B3095 occurred near Warminster at a time when that general area seemed to be a hot spot for UFO sightings and other anomalous phenomena. It is also interesting to note that there appears to be a history of psychic experiences in Amanda's extended family. Given that Amanda's mother developed a chronic problem with blisters shortly after the encounter on the B3095, it's possible that she was exposed to some sort of harmful radiation. More speculatively, one might wonder whether the incident had some bearing on Amanda's developing multiple sclerosis.

VEHICLE INTERFERENCE

There are cases on record in which vehicles have developed mysterious malfunctions, or where the drivers have experienced difficulty in controlling them. I've already mentioned some incidents of this type. For example, in the last chapter, I referred to the malfunctioning of Christine Smith's car in conjunction with a UFO experience on the A65 in North Yorkshire. With two exceptions, this chapter will look at cases of vehicle interference that *don't* seem to have involved a UFO sighting, although, in some instances, strange mists or clouds played a prominent role, and seemingly had a marked effect on the occupant(s) of the vehicle. Of course, it may be that there's no fundamental difference between cases featuring UFOs, on the one hand, and clouds or mists, on the other, since what some witnesses would call a 'cloud' or 'mist' might be interpreted by others as a UFO.

This chapter also includes a case in which a car was found in the middle of a muddy field after the driver turned up, on foot, some miles away, with no memory of how he'd got there.

NO UFO OR STRANGE CLOUD/MIST REPORTED

I'll start by citing cases where there's no explicit mention of UFOs or strange clouds or mists.

The legend of the 'hairy hands', Dartmoor

Since around 1910, according to a *Wikipedia* article, there have been reports of people having unusual accidents on Dartmoor, between Postbridge and Two Bridges, with many of the victims stating that their vehicle had jolted or swerved violently and gone off the road, as if something had wrenched the wheel out of the driver's control.[1] The article states that Dr E.H. Helby, the medical officer for Dartmoor Prison, lost control of his motorcycle combination in June 1921 and was killed, although two girls in the sidecar, daughters of the prison governor, survived. (Other sources describe the girls as Helby's own daughters.) The article reports that several weeks later, a coach driver lost control, with a number of passengers being thrown out of their seats and injured. And it states that an army captain claimed that a pair of invisible hands had seized him, forcing him and his motorcycle off the road in August 1921.

In his booklet *Supernatural Dartmoor*, Michael Williams refers to a journalist, Rufus Endle, who had allegedly regarded the story of the hairy hands as 'pure legend' until experiencing the phenomenon himself at Postbridge one night.[2] A pair of hands gripped his steering wheel as he approached the bridge, whereupon he had to fight for control. It was, Endle stated, 'a very scary minute or so', but he managed to avoid crashing, and the ghostly hands 'went as inexplicably as they came'. It's not clear from Williams' booklet whether Endle actually saw the hands – he may have simply felt their presence. He explained that he'd not previously told anyone of his experience, for fear of ridicule, and he asked Williams not to mention it until after he (Endle) was 'dead and gone'. Unfortunately, Williams doesn't give the month and year of the alleged incident. The bridge mentioned by Endle may have been the one that crosses the East Dart River in Postbridge itself, or the one that crosses Cherry Brook, about one and a half miles to the south-west. It's not clear from Williams' reporting of this matter whether the ghostly hands appeared to be hairy.

Williams (p. 18) relates that a Sally Jones learned of a similar occurrence. Her informant, a doctor from Somerset (unnamed by Williams), didn't actually see anything unusual, but reportedly became aware of a powerful force that made the steering wheel of his car 'go wild' at Postbridge. Williams mentions the year 1977, but his wording is confusing, and it's not clear whether the incident is supposed to have occurred then. It's possible, of course, that Rufus Endle and the anonymous Somerset doctor were spinning yarns.

The aforementioned *Wikipedia* article explains that the camber of the road was dangerous in places, and was therefore changed. It also notes that sceptics have suggested that most of the accidents resulted from people, unfamiliar with the area, driving too fast.

Vehicle breakdowns near Colloway Clump, Warminster

As noted in Chapters 3 and 7, Colloway Clump is a hill copse on the north side of Warminster, Wiltshire. The late Arthur Shuttlewood referred to a Major William Hill, whose car engine cut out in that vicinity on the evening of 7 September 1965. According to Shuttlewood, as the vehicle came to a halt, its chassis shuddered under vibrations in the air. The convulsions subsided somewhat and the driver got out of the car, 'but he was immediately conscious of air vibrations of a violent character which surrounded and beat down on him, and [he] heard a sinister whining and crackling'. This rather ornate wording is typical of the way that Shuttlewood wrote. Hill reportedly checked a few things, but found nothing to account for the breakdown. But in less than 3 minutes, everything was back to normal and he was able to drive away. No UFO was seen. However, Hill estimated that the cloud layer was then at 1,500ft. Accordingly, if an aerial object had been present, it could have been obscured. The car was thoroughly inspected by skilled mechanics the next morning, but was found to be in excellent condition. Shuttlewood states that there were at least eight engine stopping incidents in that location in 1965.[3]

Incidents near Clapham Wood, West Sussex

According to a book entitled *The Demonic Connection*, which was first published in 1987, a part of West Sussex became the setting for strange and sinister events in the 1960s.[4] I'm referring to an area on the South Downs that includes Clapham Wood (near the coastal town of Worthing), Chanctonbury Ring (the site of an ancient hill fort, about 4 miles north-east of Clapham Wood) and Cissbury Ring (the site of another hill fort, about 2 miles east-north-east of Clapham Wood). Toyne Newton is the only author named on the cover of the 1987 (hardback) edition of *The Demonic Connection*, although the title page refers to 'Toyne Newton *with* Charles Walker & Alan Brown' (my emphasis). However, all three names appear on both the cover and the title page of the 1993 (paperback) edition, without the word 'with' linking Newton's name with the others. Presumably, then, Walker and Brown are to be regarded as co-authors of the 1993 edition, although the text (which implies that there's only one author) hasn't been updated. The only other difference between the 1987 and 1993 editions is that the latter contains fewer photographs than the first edition.

The claims made about this part of West Sussex are controversial, with *The Demonic Connection* suggesting that a black magic group has used Clapham Wood for occult rituals. However, there may be normal, non-paranormal explanations for much of what has been reported. I've analysed the case in some detail in Chapter 6 of my book *Zones of Strangeness*. I'll confine myself here to mentioning vehicle problems that drivers allegedly had in the vicinity in past years. I'm not aware of any recent reports.

According to *The Demonic Connection* (p. 19), motorists had sometimes felt their steering wheels being pulled round in the direction of Clapham Wood while travelling along the nearby A27. The book mentions two particular drivers – a down-to-earth builder and a nursing sister – who had experienced the phenomenon. It also states (p. 24) that drivers on

Clapham Wood, near Worthing, West Sussex.

A pentagram carved into a tree stump in Clapham Wood.

the Longfurlong (the part of the A280 that runs along the west and north sides of Clapham Wood) had often claimed that their engines had become temporarily faulty, or that their cars' electrical circuits had behaved erratically.[5] The authors refer to an incident, in December 1982, involving a driver who swerved into a hedgerow when his car's engine suddenly caught fire. But they note that verification of such incidents is never easy.

A building contractor's experience

Peter Hough and Jenny Randles refer to a building contractor, Peter Taylor, who regularly drove through Daresbury, Cheshire, 'in winter 1973'. That could mean either the early part of 1973 or its last few weeks, both of which would have been winter. Anyway, according to Hough and Randles, on two successive nights, Taylor's 2-month-old car broke down as he passed The Ring O' Bells inn. He pushed the car 'down the hill' (Hough and Randles' words) and it started again on both occasions. But this puzzles me slightly, because I've visited the inn, and the road outside is fairly level. At any rate, the authors state that nothing was found to be wrong when Taylor's vehicle was subsequently checked. A few days after the second breakdown, he left work at 7.30 p.m. and again had a temporary problem with his car in Daresbury, although Hough and Randles don't say whether it happened at the same spot as before. Then, Taylor discovered that he was lost. He found a telephone box. Looking at the dial, he learned that he was in Preston, Lancashire. It was 9.30 p.m., and he was unable to account for the large amount of time that had passed. But thereafter, his car ran well.[6]

It appears that Taylor wasn't the only person to report puzzling car breakdowns in the area. Hough and Randles (p. 89) relate that in the summer of 1988, a woman informed them that her car had temporarily broken down a few hundred yards from the physics laboratory near Daresbury, although nothing was found to be wrong with it when it was checked. The authors make no mention of missing time in connection with that incident. The woman hadn't heard of Taylor's experiences, but she'd been told of other cars having similar problems on the same road (the one on which her car had

The Ring O' Bells inn, Daresbury.

malfunctioned, presumably). She wondered whether it was related to some sort of experiment at the lab.

ENGINE FAILURE AT LANGENHOE, ESSEX

In the early hours of 14 September 1965, Paul Green, a 29-year-old engineer, was riding a motorcycle home to West Mersea after visiting his fiancée in Colchester. He heard a high-pitched humming to his left, which became louder. He noticed a pinpoint of blue light over Brightlingsea, to the east. It was winking and rapidly became larger. He realised that it was approaching him from over Langenhoe marsh. The humming increased greatly in volume and then changed to a high-pitched buzz. His motorcycle engine started to falter and then cut out, as did his lights. At this stage, he estimated, the blue flashing light was about a mile away. An enormous object loomed into view. There seemed to be a dome on top, with a flashing blue light inside. As the UFO slowly descended, it tilted. Its underside was rimmed with numerous round objects. Green walked a few paces towards it and felt spellbound. The flashing light became painfully intense. It seemed to fluctuate in rhythm with his heart and hit against his chest. He felt himself tingling all over. Then the buzzing became quieter, and the object descended in an area called Wick, where there were several farmhouses.

A scooter, which Green had overtaken earlier, approached. Its engine 'coughed' and cut out, and its rider dismounted and stood petrified, staring at the light. Green's head started throbbing and he felt as if there were a tightening band around it. With much effort, he was able to move. He pushed his motorcycle along the road and the engine fired, whereupon he mounted it and sped away. It was nearly 2 a.m. when he arrived home. Since the distance between Langenhoe and West Mersea is only about 3 miles, and given that the UFO sighting had begun about 1 a.m., Green may have experienced missing time. He reported that the following day – he may have meant later that same day – his hair and clothes seemed to be charged with electricity. Around the time of the incident, a friend of his, who lived at Shrub End, some 5 miles from Wick, reportedly saw a large, blue light passing overhead in a north-westerly direction.[7]

It may be purely coincidental, but the church of St Mary the Virgin at Langenhoe has a long history of ghostly phenomena.[8] Built in the fourteenth century, it suffered damage in an earthquake in 1884, and was demolished in

1962. The Rev. Ernest Merryweather, who was inducted as rector in 1937 and served there until his retirement from the ministry in 1959, witnessed many incidents (e.g. the displacement of objects, thudding noises, sounds of singing and footsteps, voices and apparitions). But he wasn't the only person to experience strange phenomena there. For example, there was an occasion when he and two workmen heard singing coming from the empty church.

CASES INVOLVING STRANGE CLOUDS OR MISTS

Incidents near Northampton

Jenny Randles mentions two interesting cases from villages near Northampton.[9] Driving through Little Houghton one night in September 1973, 21-year-old Paul (surname not specified) noticed that the church clock gave the time as about 2 a.m. Thereafter, he found himself wandering on foot at Bromham, 16 miles away, with no memory of getting there. It was around 7 a.m. He was soaking wet, although it wasn't raining at that point. He found a friend who lived not far away. The latter drove Paul along the A428 towards Little Houghton, the last location that Paul could recall prior to turning up at Bromham. They found Paul's car about 5 miles from Bromham. It was in the middle of a muddy field, with no sign of tyre tracks leading from a closed gate. Two years later, he had a sudden flashback of driving out of Little Houghton and seeing a fuzzy, white glow approaching his windscreen.

The second incident occurred one evening in February 1983. A 41-year-old motorcyclist, Peter Rainbow, was rounding a bend on the A428 in Great Houghton when the engine and lights of his motorbike cut out. He tried to improvise a repair using metal foil, but it didn't work. He was about to fit a spare fuse when he noticed a white glow clinging to the ground in an adjacent field. Everything had gone quiet and he felt almost entranced. The white mist wobbled and gyrated, and then vanished in a blur. Rainbow then found that he was holding the ignition key of his motorbike, not the fuse. The engine now started normally. He rode to Little Houghton, where the church clock gave the time as 8.30 p.m. This meant that a period of 90 minutes had passed in what had seemed just moments.

The Aveley incident

The Day family (mother, father, son and two daughters) were involved in an unusual incident while driving home one evening in the autumn of 1974. The location was Aveley, Essex. The case was subsequently investigated by UFO researchers Andy Collins and Barry King, and is discussed by Jenny Randles in *Time Storms* (pp. 215–217) and, at greater length, by Albert Budden. His materialistic, but speculative, theorising about UFO and apparitional phenomena places a heavy emphasis on environmental factors such as magnetic fields.[10]

As the family drove near power lines, a low aerial light seemed to follow their car. Then, they encountered a patch of glowing, green mist. As the car entered it, sparks came from the radio. Mr Day pulled out the wires in case it caught fire. There was a bump, as if the car had dropped on to the road from mid-air, and it transpired that the Days were now inexplicably nearer their home and that it was much later than they would have thought – possibly as much as 3 hours later.

The incident seemed to mark a turning point in the lives of members of the family. For example, within 2 months of the incident, Mr Day had an unexpected nervous breakdown and had to give up his job. He was out of work until September 1975, and eventually became self-employed. His wife became more self-confident and started attending college in September 1975, something that she'd long wanted to do. The couple's son, who had been behind in his reading, came to excel in that activity. The parents and two of the children gave up eating meat. The parents developed a sharpened concern for the environment, and Mr Day stopped smoking just before Christmas 1974.

In the 3 years following the Days' encounter, there were occasions when objects disappeared without a trace from rooms in their house, or turned up a few days later, somewhere else. There were also a couple of occasions when the back door flew open unexpectedly.

A family's strange experience near Hockliffe, Bedfordshire

Another case mentioned in *Time Storms* involved a mother and father and their two young daughters – the Smith family (pp. 73–74). During the morning of 8 August 1992, they went on a shopping expedition. They were driving near

Hockliffe, Bedfordshire, when a strange mood suddenly overcame them and things became quiet. At the same time, their car became enveloped in mist. But then – very soon after, it seemed to them – things returned to normal: they were no longer in the mist, normal sounds had resumed, and other traffic could be seen. After a few moments of disorientation, it became apparent that they were in Woburn Sands, approximately 8 miles from where they'd entered the mist. They suffered some after-effects, which took a while to subside. For example, Mrs Smith kept missing the door handle when she tried to open the car door, and her husband experienced difficulty in using a petrol pump.

GENERAL COMMENTS

If Jenny Randles is right about people and their vehicles being translocated in space and time as a result of some sort of impersonal electromagnetic event, what would an observer notice if he or she managed to avoid the translocation process? Imagine, for example, that a friend of the Day family had been driving along, some distance behind them, at the time of their experience. Would the friend have seen their car suddenly blink out of existence? Similarly, if another driver had been on the road when the Days' car reappeared, some distance away and at a later hour, would this witness have been amazed to see their vehicle materialise out of thin air?

If an impersonal mechanism brings about the spatial and temporal displacement of vehicles, how do we explain the fact that they generally seem to turn up on roads? In my view, this suggests intelligent direction or orchestration rather than something mechanistic and random. Indeed, if these displacements were produced in the latter way, the vehicles could presumably turn up just about anywhere, and most likely *not* on roads – they might suddenly appear in places that would be dangerous for the occupants and other people. For example, one could imagine a vehicle turning up in a lake, or dropping on to the terraces at a crowded football stadium!

Admittedly, in one of the above-mentioned cases – that of Paul – the driver's car did turn up in an unlikely place, a muddy field. He was unable to account for several hours, but there's reason to believe that he lived through that period and hadn't been displaced in space and time by a mysterious impersonal process. The mud in the field had apparently been created by recent heavy rain. Since Paul's car was in the field, it's reasonable to infer that he'd been there at some point. Quite possibly, he drove the car into the field before it became muddy, assuming that he'd been able to open the gate. He may have then proceeded on foot to Bromham. It wasn't raining when he found himself there, but his clothes were wet, suggesting that he'd been exposed to the rain.

Again, I'd suggest that the notion of paranormally instilled false memories might provide an explanation for some of these cases. Take, for example, the experience of the Smith family. If they drove the 8 miles or so to Woburn Sands, it's unlikely that they were shrouded in mist and unable to see other traffic while covering that distance, since they would almost certainly have crashed their car. Their recollection of temporarily being in a mist may have been a false memory, and something may have prevented them from remembering how they got to Woburn Sands. Of course, another possibility is that they and their vehicle were somehow translocated from the outskirts of Hockliffe to Woburn Sands, and they didn't actually drive the intervening distance.

A MISCELLANY OF BIZARRE EXPERIENCES

Road users have reported strange experiences that don't fit within the categories discussed in the previous chapters. For example, there have been alleged sightings of mysterious animals that don't appear to have been phantom dogs or alien big cats (ABCs).

BIGFOOT SIGHTINGS ON CANNOCK CHASE

Cannock Chase has been mentioned in previous chapters. In a short Internet article, Nick Redfern mentions several reports of bigfoot-type creatures being seen on the Chase and in the surrounding area.[1,2] He notes that, in 1879, a creature described as being half-man and half-monkey was seen on a road at Ranton (about 9 miles west-north-west of Cannock Chase), and that in 1995 a woman named Jackie Houghton saw a huge, lumbering, hair-covered creature in the early hours of the morning near the village of Slitting Mill. Redfern doesn't say whether she was on a road at the time.

Redfern's article quotes an unnamed witness who, along with others, allegedly saw a bigfoot-type creature while travelling by car. Unfortunately, it's not clear from Redfern's wording when the sighting occurred. He states that the account 'surfaced' in 1998, which leaves open the possibility that the sighting itself happened in a prior year. The precise location isn't specified.

It happened on a starry night. The occupants of the car saw a tall, man-like figure, 'sort of crouching forward'. As they passed, it turned and looked straight at them. The witness quoted by Redfern estimated that the creature was about 6ft 8in tall, and had thick legs and a darkish coat.

Redfern explains that, in December 2003, local newspapers gave prominence to the story of a young man named Craig, who claimed to have seen a large, ape-like creature near Penkridge, a town close to Cannock Chase. However, Redfern doesn't say whether Craig was on a road when he saw the creature. He goes on to state that an Alec Williams was driving across the Chase at night in April 2004 when he saw a huge beast near the edge of the main road that links Cannock and Rugeley.

In his book *There's Something in the Woods*, Redfern mentions a story told to him in 2001 by a man he refers to as Mick Dodds. One night in 1986, Dodds and his wife were driving near Chartley Castle (about 5 miles north of Cannock Chase) when a huge stag ambled across the road in front of them, causing Dodds to brake hard. Then, a creature, looking like a large chimpanzee, bounded after the stag, coming on to the road from a field on the couple's right. It stopped suddenly, halfway across the road, looked at the terrified couple, and charged their car, although it backed away at the last moment. Putting the car into reverse gear, Dodds inadvertently stalled the engine. As he tried to restart it, he flooded it (the carburettor, I presume). Consequently, the couple were briefly stranded on the road. For about 20 seconds, the creature stared at Dodds and his wife. It made two further charges at the car before heading off to the left, in the direction the stag had gone. Discussing the incident with Redfern, Dodds asked whether he and his wife might have experienced some form of time displacement.[3]

Comments

It's possible, of course, that people have fabricated reports of bigfoot sightings in the Cannock Chase area, and hoaxing of a different sort could account for at least some of the sightings. Dramatically entitled 'Bigfoot almost made me lose my baby', an article in the *Cannock Chase Post* claimed, in March 2006, that, 'Police chiefs [had] hit out at the dangers posed by the spoof "Bigfoot" craze after a teenager almost lost her baby when a joker clad in a gorilla suit jumped in front of her car.' According to the article, hoaxers had been tempted by the paper's offer of a free meal for anyone who caught 'the elusive Chase Bigfoot' on film! However, there was no mention in the article of anyone being apprehended for perpetrating the supposed hoax, or of anyone admitting to it. Therefore, the notion that the sighting involved someone in a gorilla suit may have been pure conjecture.

England is highly populated, and Cannock Chase is relatively small. Therefore, if these sighting reports are genuine, it's hard to believe that the incidents involved real, flesh-and-blood creatures with no officially recognised existence in the British Isles. It seems more likely that they were transient apparitional events on a par with sightings of phantom vehicles and ghostly hitchhikers. Alternatively, paranormally-generated false memories may have given rise to the reports. In other words, although someone might genuinely believe that he or she has seen a remarkable creature, the memory of having done so could be false. It may be that a tricksterish intelligence inserts false memories in order to deceive.

There have also been alleged sightings on Cannock Chase of werewolf-type creatures, of black-eyed children, and even of an entity with combined human and pig features ('pig-man'). However, so far as I know, they haven't been commonly reported by people travelling the local roads.

A PHANTOM ROAD SEEN FROM THE SEVENOAKS BYPASS

Janet and Colin Bord refer to an unnerving experience that a woman had one night in March 1979 while driving on the Sevenoaks bypass in Kent. To the driver, Mrs Babs Davidson, the road ahead appeared blacked out, and there seemed to be another road leading away to the right. Fortunately, Mrs Davidson drove in the direction of what she knew to be the real road. Had she taken the 'phantom road', she would have wound up in the path of oncoming traffic. The Bords, who reference their source for the report as the 1 April 1979 edition of the *Sunday Express*, state that Mrs Davidson had had that experience three times in all, although they don't give dates for the other two occasions. Her experience gave rise to speculation that this perceptual affect could have been responsible for four fatal accidents since November 1977, in which drivers had swerved across the grass-covered central reservation. Experts were trying to determine whether moonlight, or the headlights of oncoming vehicles, might have created an illusion that induced drivers to go the wrong way.[4]

Wondering whether there was any additional information on this case (e.g. reports from other motorists about seeing the 'phantom road'), I searched the Internet, but came up with nothing.

HUMANOIDS

Strange figures

According to the late Arthur Shuttlewood, in January 1966, a man from Frome, who didn't want to be named, told him about an experience that he'd had that month while riding his motorbike near Shearwater, a lake south-west of Warminster, Wiltshire. At midnight, he saw three grey-clad, white-faced figures enter a hedgerow near the western side of the lake. They looked like frogmen. The informant saw noses and wide-spaced eyes, but the figures had no mouths. He thought that he'd glimpsed fair hair sticking out of the cap worn by one of them, who also had a glittering belt. The figures were very human-like, but they were shorter, the witness thought, with big shoulders, larger heads and thinner legs. The motorcyclist stopped further along, and then returned to see a large saucer of light appear from the lakeside. It rose rapidly into the sky, hovered, and then flew off towards Cley Hill, which is west of Warminster and north-north-west of Shearwater. Accompanied by Lord Bath, Shuttlewood subsequently looked for landing evidence at the western end of the lake. They came upon some shallow, round depressions in the reed beds.[5]

Seven-foot figures and scents

In another book, Shuttlewood referred to sightings of three transparent, yet clearly outlined, 7ft-tall figures 'at the bottom of the lane at Starr [Hill]', near Warminster. (NB: Starr Hill is referred to as Middle Hill on the 1:25,000 OS map of the area.) They moved, he claimed, via even, gliding motions, and had no discernible legs. He stated that an exotic fragrance permeated the air around them, and that even on cold, wintry nights the atmosphere was warmed by unusual heat waves from the areas where they congregated; and he alleged that the scent of flowers that didn't grow there would vanish when the shining figures left the site, or whenever a low-flying UFO departed from the area. Confusingly, though, he claimed that the tall figures were sighted 'at quiet times of nocturnal peace, *after* a blazing UFO [had] faded into oblivion' (my emphasis).[6]

Plants may have been responsible for at least some of the olfactory experiences reported by skywatchers. The late Ken Rogers reported that a botanist called Mollie Carey visited Starr Hill one night in August 1972 and became aware of a strong fragrance wafting in warm air currents. She came upon plants that create scents – for example, *Artemisia vulgaris* (mugwort).[7]

STRANGE EXPERIENCES ON THE KINTYRE PENINSULA

An informant related to me details of some strange events that had allegedly occurred at the southern end of the Kintyre Peninsula of western Scotland in about August 1996. I'll call her Kate, which isn't her real name. At the time, she and her then husband were renting a farmhouse in a slightly elevated position that looked down on the village of Southend. Since I have no corroborating testimony from anyone else, the story can't be judged as evidentially strong; but it may be of interest none the less.

Having been out for dinner in Campbeltown, Kate and a visiting friend were driving back to the house when they came across a stationary car. It was at an odd angle on the road. The driver's door was open, and a man's body was lying face down in the road. Kate didn't stop, which was out of character for her. Shortly before encountering this scene, she and her friend had spoken about feeling a little strange. Back at the house, they were chatting in the kitchen when Kate noticed white flashes of light circling the house, pausing at the windows. She heard someone calling her name, and asked her friend whether she could hear anything. The friend said no, but she was seeing things at the window.

There were three loud knocks on the front door. Kate opened it and stepped outside. She noticed nothing to her right, but to her left she saw a humanoid figure, about 5ft tall, standing at the end of the property. She also saw several other figures behind a drystone wall. She ran back into the house and bolted the door. Her friend was extremely distressed. The lights continued circling the house, stopping at the windows.

Kate's husband, her daughter and the friend's son were also in the house, but they slept through these proceedings. I would have liked to contact the friend, to enquire about her recollections. But according to Kate, she wouldn't have been willing to talk about what happened. Regarding the man in the road, Kate informed me that she made some enquiries, but they proved negative, and nothing was reported in the local newspaper.

Kate described other strange phenomena that had occurred in the house, such as recurrent banging noises and thumping footsteps coming from one of the bedrooms. These noises were heard on occasions throughout the whole of her occupancy (approximately 7 months). After Kate and her daughter left Kintyre, in October 1996, her husband remained at the property for a short while, and continued to hear the banging.

CONCLUSIONS

Publicised cases of people having strange experiences on Britain's roads may be just the tip of the iceberg. For a variety of reasons, incidents may go largely unreported. For example, witnesses might be reluctant to go public if they fear that their accounts will be met with incredulity or derision. On the other hand, some of the publicised reports could be mischievous inventions. On balance, though, it seems that strange incidents of one sort or another are occurring quite often on our roads. Encounters with colliding apparitions seem to be particularly common, although this doesn't, of course, mean that everyone, or the majority of people, will have such an experience.

Because comparative statistical information isn't available, it's hard to know for sure whether certain stretches of road host more strange incidents than others. But given the concentration of reports from certain areas – such as Blue Bell Hill, in north Kent, and Halsall Moss, in West Lancashire – there's at least a *prima facie* case for believing that to be the case.

In Chapter 1, I referred to the notion that seeing apparitions or hearing ghostly sounds is like watching or hearing the playback of a video recording of something that happened in the past. Arguably, though, the theatricality of many apparitional events counts against that theory. Take, for example, the phantom truck seen by Paul Devereux on the M6 motorway (mentioned in Chapter 2). It seemed to have no driver. Therefore, it's hard to believe that the sighting was a 'replay' of an actual historical event.

In cases involving UFOs and strange mists or clouds, there's sometimes evidence that the witnesses were exposed to radiation or some other form of physical energy. For example, the day after her encounter on the A65, Christine Smith reportedly discovered a rash on her back and chest (see Chapter 8). In a case mentioned below, a lorry driver in Spain was allegedly found to have an abnormally high number of lymphocytes in his blood following a UFO experience.

At the end of Chapter 3, I mentioned the possibility that encounters with colliding apparitions serve as warnings to drive carefully. However, by inducing motorists to brake or swerve suddenly, the phantom figures could actually be the cause of accidents. Indeed, accidents of that sort have been mentioned. For example, in Chapter 4, I referred to a motorcyclist who had reportedly fallen off his machine and broken a limb after seeing an apparitional figure. Of course, this raises the possibility that the intelligence behind the manifestations – if there is one – likes to frighten people and cause accidents. It's not a pleasant thought.

Certainly, if we cast an eye on poltergeist and haunting cases, there are indications of a tricksterish intelligence at work. Take, for instance, a case that I investigated in Scotland some years ago. One of the informants mentioned an occasion when he discovered that three folded £20 notes had disappeared from a metal container in his living room. When he returned to his house at lunchtime that day, three £20 notes were laid out on the coffee table! They appeared new and weren't creased. On page 13 of their book *Mysteries of the Mersey Valley*, Peter Hough and Jenny Randles refer to a Mr and Mrs Farris (pseudonyms), who had bought a corner shop in Hyde, Greater Manchester. Between 1989 and 1991, they worked to renovate the gable end. That seemed to precipitate poltergeist and apparitional phenomena. For example, at one point, Mrs Farris went out for 20 minutes and returned to find that her saucepans had been removed from the shelving and set up systematically across the kitchen, from smallest to largest, with all the handles pointing the same way, and with her wok presiding over the array!

Some of the more intriguing cases mentioned in this book involved the possible dislocation of people and their vehicles in space or time, as in the case of the Smith family, who were driving on the outskirts of Hockliffe, Bedfordshire, and then found themselves some miles away, in Woburn Sands (see Chapter 9). There have also been reports from overseas. For example, Albert Rosales cites a case, from August 2011, involving a lorry driver in Spain.[1] Passing the nuclear plant near Vandellòs in Catalonia, the driver reportedly noticed, to his left, a large bluish sphere, with something white that seemed to be moving within it. The sphere was some 3–4m above the ground and about 20m from the lorry. It followed the vehicle for approximately 3–4km, at times dipping closer to the ground. At some point, the driver noticed a strange fog or mist on the road, which seemed to get thicker as he drove on. His next recollection was of lying in a sort of cot, in an illuminated room, with three humanoids present. Suddenly, he felt great chest pain. When he tried to move, he experienced pain lower down, as if his ankles had been restrained. He later found strange, linear marks on them. The entities seemed to speak to one another. Then, one of them touched the driver's head, whereupon he found himself back at the wheel of his lorry, with the engine running and the headlights on. But feeling very ill, he stopped and got out of the vehicle. After several steps, he fell to the ground. He was allegedly found, and picked up, by another lorry driver, only a few kilometres from Valencia, and about 200km from where he'd first encountered the bluish sphere. However, that distance hadn't been registered by the odometer in his lorry. At a local hospital, he was reportedly found to have an extremely high number of lymphocytes in his blood, although no cause for that was detected. After his bizarre experience, he became very respectful of nature and more interested in science, and he supposedly displayed increased precognitive faculties. But caution is warranted regarding this report: Rosales's account of the case doesn't name the driver; the link for the cited Internet source no longer works; and Rosales doesn't indicate who investigated and compiled the story.

Aircraft pilots have also reported mysterious spatial displacements. Take, for instance, the case of Graham Sheppard (1942–2005), a British commercial pilot. He had a strange experience while flying a light aircraft – a hired Cessna 172 – in Puerto Rico in 1993.[2] His plan was to fly west from San Juan (on the north coast) to the town of Arecibo (also on the north coast), then south to the area where the Arecibo radio telescope is located, and then to proceed to Mayagüez (on the west coast), where he intended to land for a break. After arriving, uneventfully, over the area of the telescope, he spent some time filming. Then, he set course for Mayagüez Airport. He climbed to 2,200ft. After some minutes of cruising and further filming, a feeling of unease and growing confusion came over him, which turned to shock when he saw a coast parallel to his track, not at right angles, as it should have been. He soon realised that he was flying along the south coast of the island, which was very odd, not least because to have got there from the area of the radio telescope would have entailed crossing a mountain barrier, the Cordillera Central. That would have necessitated ascending to at least 3,000ft, which he hadn't done.

It's hard to know how these spatial displacements occur, although it's conceivable that they involve some sort of warping or bending of space. By way of analogy, imagine a sheet of A4 paper lying on a table, with two small circles drawn on it, one near the left-hand edge and the other near the right-hand edge, with both circles being halfway down the page (i.e. at the same level). Imagine that there's a small spider in the middle of the circle on the left of the sheet and that it wants to go to the other circle. Normally, this would require it to traverse a distance of several inches, which might take several seconds. But if someone took hold of the edges of the sheet and folded it, the two circles could be brought together. The spider would then be able to step across to the circle on the right without having to traverse a distance of several inches. By the same token, it's conceivable that the temporary warping or bending of space could bring two widely separated places together, making it possible to travel from one to the other in next to no time.

However, I'm not sure how credible such a notion is in terms of established physics. Einstein's general theory of relativity depicts gravity in terms of the bending or 'curvature' of space and time in the presence of large masses. For example, the path of a beam of light passing close to a star will be deflected slightly, because the space around the star will be somewhat curved. However, it takes a very large mass to distort the nearby space sufficiently to produce a measurable deflection of a light beam. Therefore, it's hard to see how the spatial displacements described above could be explained in 'relativistic' terms. Indeed, if massive gravitational forces were behind these phenomena, they would no doubt be detected, and the effects would be much more widespread.

I've little doubt that mysterious spatial translocations do occur, but I'm less sure about the notion that people and their vehicles can jump forward in time. If, for example, the occupants of a car encounter a strange mist and then discover that it is much later than they thought, they may have lived through a period of time for which they have no recall.

People with an interest in the paranormal often like to visit locations that have been the setting for strange phenomena. For example, during its heyday as a supposed UFO hot spot in the 1960s and 1970s, the Warminster area of Wiltshire attracted many visitors; and, to this day, Rendlesham

Forest in Suffolk is a magnet for the curious, because it has supposedly been the setting for a variety of unusual manifestations. Indeed, visitors to Rendlesham Forest might have a fair chance of experiencing something paranormal there, particularly if they're prepared to make multiple visits. But visitors to the roads mentioned in this book may be unlikely to have a paranormal encounter. Take, for example, the cases discussed in Chapter 3 concerning the B721 and A75 roads in southern Scotland. Although I've cited quite a few reports, the alleged incidents have been spread over a good many years. Therefore, unless many sightings are going unreported, the probability of experiencing anything noteworthy there at any particular time might be rather low.

NOTES

CHAPTER 1: Fundamentals

1. Rupert Sheldrake, *Dogs That Know When Their Owners Are Coming Home*.
2. G.L. Playfair, 'The twin thing', *Fortean Times*, Issue 171, June 2003, pp. 34–40.
3. Jenny Randles, *Time Storms*, p. 152.
4. Andrew MacKenzie, *Adventures in Time*, pp. 3–30.
5. See, for example, G.N.M. Tyrrell, *Apparitions*.
6. I.M. Owen and Margaret Sparrow, *Conjuring Up Philip*.
7. G.L. Playfair, *This House is Haunted*.
8. Harry Price, *Poltergeist*, pp. 43–61; pp. 388–99.
9. Melvyn Willin, *Ghosts Caught on Film*.
10. Myers' theory is discussed on pp. 45–8 of *Apparitions* by G.N.M. Tyrrell.
11. Tyrrell, op. cit., p. 110.
12. Tyrrell's book doesn't actually name the town in which the haunting occurred. A detailed examination of the case is provided by B.A. Collins in his book *The Cheltenham Ghost*. Another thoughtful exposition and analysis of the case is provided by the late Andrew MacKenzie in his book *Hauntings and Apparitions*, pp. 40–64.
13. D.S. Rogo, *Beyond Reality*, pp. 59–60.
14. H.M. Denning, *True Hauntings*, pp. 65–6.

15. Accounts of this case can be found in the following books: *Extreme Hauntings*, by Paul Adams and Eddie Brazil; *Poltergeists*, by Alan Gauld and A.D. Cornell; *Poltergeist*, by Harry Price; *Poltergeists*, by Sacheverell Sitwell.

16. Jenny Randles, *Supernatural Pennines*, pp. 30–2.

17. M.A. Persinger and S.A. Koren, 'Predicting the characteristics of haunt phenomena from geomagnetic factors and brain sensitivity: Evidence from field and experimental studies', in J. Houran & R. Lange (eds), *Hauntings and Poltergeists*, pp. 179–94. (The relevant passage is on pp. 187–9.)

18. Carol Rainey, 'The priests of high strangeness: Co-creation of the "alien abduction phenomenon"', http://www.carolrainey.com/pdf/ParatopiaMag_vol1_1-15-11.pdf

19. Budd Hopkins, 'Deconstructing the debunkers: A response', http://www.lindacortilecase.com/deconstructing-the-debunkers.html

20. Albert Budden, *Electric UFOs*, pp. 262–8.

21. Peter Hough, 'Alien abductions revisited', *Fortean Times*, 258, February 2010, pp. 55–7. A passage on p. 56 of the article states that 'abductees had a *significantly* better appraisal of their own and other people's emotions than the controls' (my emphasis). However, I understand from Peter Hough (Facebook message, January 2017) that although the abductees scored higher on this measure, the difference *wasn't*, in fact, statistically significant.

22. http://www.pauldevereux.co.uk

23. C.G. Jung, *Flying Saucers*.

24. David Deutsch, *The Fabric of Reality*.

25. F.A. Wolf, *Parallel Universes*.

CHAPTER 2: Phantom Vehicles and Aircraft

1. There's a detailed examination of the Loch Ashie phenomena in Chapter 14 of my book *Zones of Strangeness*.

2. C.J. Shaw, *A History of Clan Shaw*, p. 270.

3. Peter Underwood, *Gazetteer of Scottish Ghosts*, p. 177.

4. It appears that Paterson's father and mother may also have seen the locomotive. His aunt had been in the car as well, but she was apparently unsure whether she'd seen it.

5. Gandy described these two sightings in a short article, 'The old man of Halsall Moss', *Fortean Times*, 56, 1990, pp. 52–3. He also mentions these sightings, along with other reports, in an article, with the same title, in a much more recent issue of the magazine (see below).

6. Rob Gandy, 'The old man of Halsall Moss', *Fortean Times*, 328, June 2015, pp. 32–9.

7. David Clarke, *Supernatural Peak District*, pp. 150–1. (Clarke's source for this report is apparently W.A. Boylan's *Derbyshire Ghosts*.)

8. Alan Baker, *Ghosts and Spirits*, pp. 37–8.

9. Paul Devereux, *Haunted Land*, pp. 140–2.

10. 'A3 Burpham Ghost Crash (2002)', http://www.mysteriousbritain. co.uk/england/surrey/hauntings/a3-burpham-ghost-crash-2002.html

CHAPTER 3: Colliding Apparitions

1. Neil Fraser-Tytler, *Extracts from Tales of Old Days on the Aldourie Estate*, p. 5. A copy of this booklet is available in the reference section of Inverness Library (shelf no. 941.21). It can also be downloaded via: http://southlochnessheritage.co.uk/wp-content/uploads/2014/08/ Tales-from.pdf

2. C.J. Shaw, *A History of Clan Shaw*, p. 270.

3. 'Scottish Folklore: The Ghosts of the Kinmount Straight', https:// modern.scot/ghosts-of-kinmount-straight-2

4. Andrew Green, 'Ghosts in Scotland and the North United Kingdom' (the item appears under the sub-heading 'Gretna Green'), http:// www.mystical-www.co.uk/index.php?option=com_content&view =article&id=181&Itemid=261

5. Peter Underwood, *Gazetteer of Scottish Ghosts*, pp. 14–17.

6. 'Dumfries bypass', http://www.mysteriousbritain.co.uk/scotland/ dumfriesshire/hauntings/dumfries-bypass.html

7. 'The A75 Kinmount straight: Trip on "most haunted" road', http:// www.bbc.co.uk/news/uk-scotland-south-scotland-24655488

8. Rob Gandy, 'The old man of Halsall Moss', *Fortean Times*, 328, June 2015, pp. 32–9.

9. Kirst D'Raven and Steve Mera, 'The Stocksbridge bypass: A critical analysis', *Phenomena Magazine*, Issue 21, January 2011, pp. 13–18, http://www.phenomenamagazine.co.uk/cgi-bin/download.cgi

10. David Clarke, *Supernatural Peak District*, pp. 33–4.
11. 'Dangerous driving', https://www.theguardian.com/lifeandstyle/2002/sep/22/foodanddrink.restaurants
12. Sean Tudor has done considerable research on road ghost cases, and his website contains interesting information: 'Road ghosts', http://www.roadghosts.com/Introduction.htm. For details about the A15 apparitions, click on 'Cases – UK' on the left-hand side of the introductory page and then scroll down to 'Lincolnshire: Ruskington (revised)'.
13. Sean Tudor was apparently in touch with this witness by email. He states on his website that she reported that the week after her sighting, cutlery in her cupboard, and her car keys, had twisted!
14. The website of LincsPRT is http://www.lincsprt.com
15. Lee Brickley, *UFOs Werewolves & the Pig-Man*, pp. 100–3.
16. Carolyn and David Taylor, 'Roads to the otherworld: Contemporary haunted roads and a sacred landscape', http://www.mysteriousbritain.co.uk/england/west-midlands/hauntings/roads-to-the-otherworld-contemporary-haunted-roads-and-a-sacred-landscape.html
17. I understand from David Taylor that the names given to the witnesses in the article are pseudonyms.
18. This may be a pseudonym.
19. Jeremy Harte, 'Haunted roads', *The Ley Hunter*, 121, 1994, pp. 1–7.
20. Harte's wording isn't very precise: some of the seventy or so 'hauntings' that he lists appear to have entailed only auditory phenomena.
21. Janet and Colin Bord, *Modern Mysteries of Britain*, pp. 35–6.
22. Sean Tudor, 'Hit and myth', *Fortean Times*, 73, 1994, pp. 27–31; Sean Tudor, 'Hell's belles', *Fortean Times*, 104, 1997, pp. 36–40.
23. Steve Dewey and John Ries, *In Alien Heat*.
24. See: 'White Hill', http://www.roadghosts.com/CasesUKaccounts.htm. It references an article entitled 'Coach driver's ghostly collision' by Sally Yonish, *Kentish Express*, 13 January 2000, p. 3.
25. John Rackham, *Brighton Ghosts, Hove Hauntings*, pp. 305–7.

CHAPTER 4: Phantom Hitchhikers

1. Michael Goss, *The Evidence for Phantom Hitch Hikers*, p. 13.
2. 'Is this the ghost of an RAF pilot killed in the Second World War? Motorists believe the spirit of the dead airman was trying to thumb a lift', http://www.dailymail.co.uk/news/article-3192105/Is-ghost-RAF-pilot-killed-WW2-Motorists-believe-spirit-dead-airman-trying-thumb-lift.html#ixzz4R2Et5gGS
3. 'Phantom hitchhiker could be ghost of RAF pilot killed in crash, say terrified drivers', http://www.mirror.co.uk/news/weird-news/phantom-hitchhiker-could-ghost-raf-6215131
4. Rob Gandy, 'The old man of Halsall Moss', *Fortean Times*, 328, June 2015, pp. 32–9.
5. 'Haunted roads in Southport and west Lancashire', http://www.southportgb.co.uk/showthread.php?t=50681681&page=1
6. Lee Brickley, *UFOs Werewolves & the Pig-Man*, pp. 90–6.
7. Goss's wording is ambiguous. It could mean that the girl would get out of the car and then vanish in the vicinity of Week Street. Alternatively, it could mean that she would vanish from the car itself when it was in that area. I presume that Goss meant the latter.
8. However, Goss (pp. 103–4) goes on to indicate that Harber had allegedly interviewed a witness who had encountered the girl in 1966. The interview had supposedly occurred less than twenty-four hours after the incident.
9. But later (p. 109), Goss states that Harber told a journalist that the incidents usually occurred *after* 11 p.m.
10. Goss (p. 106) gives the age of the bride-to-be as 22, but Sean Tudor ascertained that she was in fact 24.
11. Studholme moved to New York in 1977, aged about 26. Therefore, he must have been born around 1951. See: http://www.richardstudholme.com/biog.htm
12. 'A38 Willand to Taunton road', http://www.roadghosts.com/CasesUKaccounts.htm

CHAPTER 5: Alien Big Cats

1. Janet and Colin Bord, *Modern Mysteries of Britain*, p. 100.
2. Merrily Harpur, *Mystery Big Cats*, p. 103.
3. Anonymous, 'The great Essex lion flap', *Fortean Times*, 293, October 2012, pp. 4–5.
4. Merrily Harpur, op. cit., pp. 24–5. (Harpur, p. 116, mistakenly describes Shooters Hill as being in Essex.)
5. Redfern wrote the article, entitled 'Weirdness in the woods: Strange creatures of Rendlesham Forest', for a now-defunct magazine called *Beyond*. He didn't receive any printed copies of the issue containing the article; therefore, he doesn't know which issue it appeared in, or whether the title was changed. It may have been published in 2008.
6. Janet and Colin Bord, op. cit., pp. 107–8.
7. Merrily Harpur, op. cit., p. 167.
8. Merrily Harpur, ibid., p. 2.
9. Merrily Harpur, ibid., p. 1.
10. Merrily Harpur, ibid., pp. 34–7.

CHAPTER 6: Phantom Black Dogs

1. Simon Sherwood, 'Apparitions of black dogs', *Paranormal Review*, 22, April 2002, pp. 3–6.
2. Janet and Colin Bord, *Modern Mysteries of Britain*, pp. 44–5.
3. Janet and Colin Bord, ibid., pp. 43–4.
4. Janet and Colin Bord, ibid., p. 45.
5. Janet and Colin Bord, ibid., pp. 45–6.
6. Simon Sherwood, 'A psychological approach to apparitions of black dogs', in Bob Trubshaw (ed.), *Explore Phantom Black Dogs*, pp. 21–35 (the relevant passages are on pages 21 and 28).
7. Janet and Colin Bord, op. cit., p. 47.
8. Janet and Colin Bord, ibid., p. 47.
9. Nigel Mortimer, 'Appletreewick revisited…', *UFO DATA Magazine*, May/June 2008, pp. 65–7.
10. Christopher Reeve, *A Straunge and Terrible Wunder*, p. 42.

11. Jennifer Westwood, 'Friend or foe? Norfolk traditions of Shuck', in Bob Trubshaw (ed.), *Explore Phantom Black Dogs*, pp. 57–76 (the relevant passage is on p. 66).

12. Alan Murdie, 'Ghost Club lecture: Mark Norman's Black Dogs', *The Ghost Club Journal*, Issue 3, 2015, pp. 24–5.

13. Jeremy Harte, 'Black Dog studies', in Bob Trubshaw (ed.), *Explore Phantom Black Dogs*, pp. 5–20 (the relevant passage is on p. 18).

CHAPTER 7: Mysterious Light Phenomena and UFOs

1. Paul Devereux, *Earth Lights Revelation*, p. 91.

2. David Clarke, *Supernatural Peak District*, pp. 136–7.

3. Paul Devereux, op. cit., p. 91.

4. Clarke (p. 136) quotes her as saying that the light 'lit up all the bottom half of the mountain' along with the railway, reservoirs and about 2 miles of road. Devereux (p. 91) states that she told Clarke that the whole mountainside was lit up, from Shining Clough across to Black Hill.

5. David Clarke, op. cit., pp. 131–2.

6. Jenny Randles, *Supernatural Pennines*, pp. 203–5.

7. Ron Halliday, *UFO Scotland*, pp. 187–8.

8. Steve Mera and Steve Yarwood, 'The Carrington UFOs', *Phenomena Magazine*, Issue 6, October 2009. Available for free download at: http://www.phenomenamagazine.co.uk/cgi-bin/download.cgi

9. Peter Hough and Jenny Randles, *Mysteries of the Mersey Valley*, pp. 35–6.

10. Arthur Shuttlewood, *The Warminster Mystery*, pp. 59–61.

11. Steve Dewey and John Ries, *In Alien Heat*, pp. 292–4.

12. Brad Steiger, *Strangers from the Skies*, p. 78.

13. Arthur Shuttlewood, *Warnings from Flying Friends*, pp. 61–3.

14. R.J. Pugh and F.W. Holiday, *The Dyfed Enigma*, pp. 44–7.

15. Michael Williams, *Supernatural Dartmoor*, pp. 20–1.

CHAPTER 8: UFO Experiences Involving 'Missing Time'

1. Malcolm Robinson, 'Abducted on the A70…', *UFO DATA Magazine*, March–April 2007, pp. 33–43.
2. Ron Halliday, *UFO Scotland*, pp. 214–17.
3. Jenny Randles, *Time Storms*, pp. 218–20.
4. Ron Halliday, op. cit., pp. 210–13.
5. Carl Nagaitis and Philip Mantle, *Without Consent*, pp. 45–53.
6. Paul Devereux, *Earth Lights Revelation*, pp. 112–13.
7. Tony Dodd, *Alien Investigator*, pp. 62–6; p. 119 (it's on page 64 where Dodd reports that she didn't feel afraid during the journey).
8. A YouTube clip from the programme used to be available, but has now been withdrawn.
9. Sam Willey, 'The High Bentham Incident', http://www.unexplained-mysteries.com/column.php?id=85560
10. Jenny Randles, *The Pennine UFO Mystery*, pp. 122–69.
11. 'U.F.O. in Todmorden Part 1, Alien Abduction', http://www.youtube.com/watch?v=iOJiwS6YMtk; 'U.F.O. in Todmorden Part 2, Alien Abduction', http://www.youtube.com/watch?v=pAc41UINwts&feature=related; 'U.F.O. in Todmorden Part 3, Alien Abduction', http://www.youtube.com/watch?v=GLNWogVLuHI&feature=rel
12. Peter Brookesmith, David Clarke and Andy Roberts, 'A policeman's lot: Part 2', *Fortean Times*, 270, January 2011, pp. 46–9.
13. Paul Weatherhead, *Weird Calderdale*, p. 45.
14. Peter Hough and Jenny Randles, *Mysteries of the Mersey Valley*, pp. 85–104.
15. Jenny Randles, 'Aerial buzzes and humming hills', *Fortean Times*, 273, April 2011, p. 27.
16. Peter Hough and Jenny Randles, op. cit., pp. 94–5.

CHAPTER 9: Vehicle Interference

1. 'Hairy hands', http://en.wikipedia.org/wiki/Hairy_hands
2. Michael Williams, *Supernatural Dartmoor*, pp. 18–19.
3. Arthur Shuttlewood, *The Warminster Mystery*, pp. 93–5.

4. Toyne Newton, Charles Walker and Alan Brown, *The Demonic Connection*.

5. The Ordnance Survey map of the area spells 'Longfurlong' as one word. *The Demonic Connection* renders it as 'Long Furlong'.

6. Peter Hough and Jenny Randles, *Mysteries of the Mersey Valley*, pp. 88–9.

7. B.E. Finch, 'The Langenhoe Incident (Motorcyclist encounters UFO)', http://www.ufoevidence.org/cases/case631.htm (Regarding the place called 'Wick' mentioned in this report, I wonder whether the witness was referring to Fingringhoe Wick.)

8. Paul Adams and Eddie Brazil, *Extreme Hauntings*, pp. 64–71.

9. Jenny Randles, *Time Storms*, pp. 22–3.

10. Albert Budden, *Electric UFOs*, p. 124; pp. 141–9; pp. 151–2; p. 193.

CHAPTER 10: A Miscellany of Bizarre Experiences

1. Many writers spell 'bigfoot' with a capital 'B', but since the word is used as a common noun, I prefer to render it with a lower-case 'b'.

2. Nick Redfern, 'In Search of the British Bigfoot', http://cryptomundo.com/bigfoot-report/british-bigfoot/

3. Nick Redfern, *There's Something in the Woods*, pp. 24–5.

4. Janet and Colin Bord, *Modern Mysteries of Britain*, p. 118; p. 307.

5. Arthur Shuttlewood, *The Warminster Mystery*, pp. 156–7.

6. Arthur Shuttlewood, *More UFOs over Warminster*, pp. 4–6.

7. Ken Rogers, *The Warminster Triangle*, p. 96.

CHAPTER 11: Conclusions

1. A.S. Rosales, *Humanoid Encounters 2010-2015*, pp. 56–7.

2. Timothy Good, *Unearthly Disclosure*, pp. 31–8.

BIBLIOGRAPHY

Adams, P. & Brazil, E. (2013). *Extreme Hauntings: Britain's Most Terrifying Ghosts*. Brimscombe Port, Stroud: The History Press.

Anonymous (2012). The great Essex lion flap. *Fortean Times*, 293, pp. 4–5.

Baker, A. (1998). *Ghosts and Spirits*. London: Orion Media.

Bord, J. & Bord, C. (1988). *Modern Mysteries of Britain: One Hundred Years of Strange Events*. London: Grafton Books.

Boylan, W.A. (1992). *Derbyshire Ghosts*. Derby: J.H. Hall & Sons.

Brickley, L. (2013). *UFOs Werewolves & the Pig-Man: Exposing England's Strangest Location – Cannock Chase*. Yam Yam Books.

Brookesmith, P., Clarke, D. & Roberts, A. (2011). A policeman's lot: Part 2. *Fortean Times*, 270, 46–49.

Budden, A. (1998). *Electric UFOs: Fireballs, Electromagnetics and Abnormal States*. London: Blandford.

Clarke, D. (2000). *Supernatural Peak District*. London: Robert Hale.

Collins, B.A. (1948). *The Cheltenham Ghost*. London: Psychic Press.

Denning, H.M. (1996). *True Hauntings: Spirits with a Purpose*. St Paul, Minnesota: Llewellyn Publications.

Deutsch, D. (1998). *The Fabric of Reality*. London: Penguin Books.

Devereux, P. (1990) (with Clarke, D., Roberts, A. & McCartney, P.). *Earth Lights Revelation: UFOs and Mystery Lightform Phenomena – The Earth's Secret Energy Force*. London: Blandford.

Devereux, P. (2001). *Haunted Land: Investigations into Ancient Mysteries and Modern Day Phenomena*. London: Piatkus.

Dewey, S. & Ries, J. (2006). *In Alien Heat: The Warminster Mystery Revisited*. San Antonio, Texas: Anomalist Books.

Dodd, T. (1999). *Alien Investigator: The Case Files of Britain's Leading UFO Detective*. London: Headline.

Fontana, D. (2005). *Is There an Afterlife?* Ropley, Hants.: O Books.

Fraser-Tytler, N. (*c.*1924). *Extracts from Tales of Old Days on the Aldourie Estate.* Available in the reference section of Inverness Library (shelf no. 941.21). (Also available online, at: http://www.southlochnessheritage. co.uk/uploads/files/Tales%20from.pdf)

Gandy, R. (1990). The old man of Halsall Moss, *Fortean Times*, 56, pp. 52–53.

Gandy, R. (2015). The old man of Halsall Moss. *Fortean Times*, 328, pp. 32–39.

Gauld, A. & Cornell, A.D. (1979). *Poltergeists.* London: Routledge & Kegan Paul.

Good, T. (2001). *Unearthly Disclosure: Conflicting Interests in the Control of Extraterrestrial Intelligence.* London: Arrow Books.

Goss, M. (1984). *The Evidence for Phantom Hitch-Hikers.* Wellingborough, Northamptonshire: The Aquarian Press.

Green, A. (1980). *Ghosts of Today.* London: Kaye & Ward.

Halliday, R. (1998). *UFO Scotland.* Edinburgh: B&W Publishing.

Harpur, M. (2006). *Mystery Big Cats.* Wymeswold, Loughborough: Heart of Albion Press.

Harte, J. (1994). Haunted roads. *The Ley Hunter*, 121, pp. 1–7.

Harte, J. (2005). Black Dog studies. In B. Trubshaw (ed.). *Explore Phantom Black Dogs.* Avebury, Marlborough: Explore Books/Heart of Albion. (pp. 5–20).

Hopkins, B. (1983). *Missing Time: A Documented Study of UFO Abductions.* New York: Berkley Books. (First published in 1981.)

Hough, P. (2010). Alien abductions revisited. *Fortean Times*, 258, pp. 55–57.

Hough, P. & Randles, J. (1993). *Mysteries of the Mersey Valley.* Wilmslow: Sigma Leisure.

Houran, J. & Lange, R. (eds), *Hauntings and Poltergeists: Multidisciplinary Perspectives.* Jefferson, North Carolina: McFarland.

Jung, C.G. (2002). *Flying Saucers: A Modern Myth of Things Seen in the Sky.* London: Routledge Classics. (First published in English in 1959.)

McCue, P.A. (2012). *Zones of Strangeness: An Examination of Paranormal and UFO Hot Spots.* Bloomington, Indiana: AuthorHouse.

MacKenzie, A. (1982). *Hauntings and Apparitions.* London: Heinemann.

MacKenzie, A. (1997). *Adventures in Time: Encounters with the Past.* London: Athlone Press.

Mortimer, N. (2008). Appletreewick revisited ... *UFO DATA Magazine*, May/June, pp. 65–67.

Murdie, A. (2015). Ghost Club lecture: Mark Norman's Black Dogs. *The Ghost Club Journal*, Issue 3, pp. 24–25.

Nagaitis, C. & Mantle, P. (2002). *Without Consent*. Leeds: Beyond Publications.

Newton, T., Walker, C. & Brown, A. (1993). *The Demonic Connection: An Investigation into Satanism in England and the International Black Magic Conspiracy*. Worthing: Badgers Books. (First published in 1987 by Blandford Press.)

Owen, I.M. & Sparrow, M. (1976). *Conjuring Up Philip: An Adventure in Psychokinesis*. New York: Harper & Row.

Persinger, M.A. & Koren, S.A. (2001). Predicting the characteristics of haunt phenomena from geomagnetic factors and brain sensitivity: Evidence from field and experimental studies. In J. Houran & R. Lange (eds), *Hauntings and Poltergeists: Multidisciplinary Perspectives*. Jefferson, North Carolina: McFarland, pp. 179–194.

Playfair, G.L. (1980). *This House is Haunted: An Investigation of the Enfield Poltergeist*. London: Souvenir Press.

Playfair, G.L. (2003). The twin thing. *Fortean Times*, 171, pp. 34–40.

Price, H. (1993). *Poltergeist: Tales of the Supernatural*. London: Bracken Books. (First published as *Poltergeist over England* by Country Life in 1945.)

Pugh, R.J. & Holiday, F.W. (1979). *The Dyfed Enigma: Unidentified Flying Objects in West Wales*. London: Faber and Faber.

Rackham, J. (2001). *Brighton Ghosts, Hove Hauntings: True Ghost Stories from Brighton, Hove and Neighbouring Villages*. Brighton: Latimer Publications.

Radin, D. (2006). *Entangled Minds: Extrasensory Experiences in a Quantum Reality*. New York: Paraview Pocket Books.

Randles, J. (1983). *The Pennine UFO Mystery*. St Albans: Granada.

Randles, J. (2001). *Time Storms: Amazing Evidence for Time Warps, Space Rifts and Time Travel*. London: Piatkus.

Randles, J. (2002). *Supernatural Pennines*. London: Robert Hale.

Randles, J. (2011). Aerial buzzes and humming hills. *Fortean Times*, 273, p. 27.

Redfern, N. (2008). *There's Something in the Woods: A Transatlantic Hunt for Monsters and the Mysterious*. San Antonio, Texas: Anomalist Books.

Reeve, C. (1988). *A Straunge and Terrible Wunder: The Story of the Black Dog of Bungay*. Bungay, Suffolk: Morrow & Co.

Robinson, M. (2007). Abducted on the A70 … *UFO DATA Magazine.* March–April, pp. 33–43.

Rogers, K. (1994). *The Warminster Triangle.* Warminster: Coates & Parker.

Rogo, D.S. (1990). *Beyond Reality: The Role Unseen Dimensions Play in Our Lives.* Wellingborough: Aquarian Press.

Rosales, A.S. (2016). *Humanoid Encounters 2010-2015: The Others Amongst Us.* Triangulum Publishing.

Shaw, C.J. (1983). *A History of Clan Shaw.* Chichester: Phillimore.

Sheldrake, R. (2011). *Dogs That Know When Their Owners Are Coming Home: And Other Unexplained Powers of Animals.* New York: Broadway Books. (First published in 1999.)

Sherwood, S. (2002). Apparitions of black dogs. *Paranormal Review*, 22, pp. 3–6.

Sherwood, S. (2005). A psychological approach to apparitions of black dogs. In B. Trubshaw (ed.). *Explore Phantom Black Dogs.* Avebury, Marlborough: Explore Books/Heart of Albion, pp. 21–35.

Shuttlewood, A. (1968). *Warnings from Flying Friends.* Warminster: Portway Press.

Shuttlewood, A. (1973). *The Warminster Mystery.* London: Universal-Tandem Publishing. (First published by Neville Spearman, London, in 1967.)

Shuttlewood, A. (1979). *More UFOs over Warminster.* London: Arthur Barker.

Sitwell, S. (1988). *Poltergeists: An Introduction and Examination followed by Chosen Instances.* New York: Dorset Press. (First published in 1959.)

Steiger, B. (1970). *Strangers from the Skies.* London: Tandem.

Tudor, S. (1994). Hit and Myth. *Fortean Times*, 73, pp. 27–31.

Tudor, S. (1997). Hell's Belles. *Fortean Times*, 104, pp. 36–40.

Tudor, S. (2017). *The Ghosts of Blue Bell Hill & other Road Ghosts: A Case-centred Study of Phantom Hitch-Hikers & Phantom Jaywalkers in Folklore and Fact.* White Ladies Press. Available via Lulu and Amazon.

Tyrrell, G.N.M. (1973). *Apparitions.* London: Society for Psychical Research. (First published in 1943.)

Underwood, P. (1980). *Gazetteer of Scottish Ghosts.* Glasgow: Fontana/Collins.

Vallee, J. (2008). *Revelations: Alien Contact and Human Deception.* San Antonio, Texas: Anomalist Books. (First published in 1991.)

Weatherhead, P. (2004). *Weird Calderdale.* Hebden Bridge: Tom Bell Publishing.

Westwood, J. (2005). Friend or foe? Norfolk traditions of Shuck. In B. Trubshaw (ed.). *Explore Phantom Black Dogs*. Avebury, Marlborough: Explore Books/Heart of Albion, pp. 57–76.

Williams, M. (2003). *Supernatural Dartmoor*. Langore, Launceston: Bossiney Books.

Willin, M. (2007). *Ghosts Caught on Film: Photographs of the Paranormal*. Cincinnati, Ohio: David & Charles.

Wolf, F.A. (1991). *Parallel Universes: The Search for Other Worlds*. London: Paladin.

INDEX